Between Earth and Heaven

A beginner's guide to living a spiritual life

by Kristi Pederson

Graphics and layout by Roxanne Wach
Original cover photo by Angie Montgomery

ISBN: 978-0-578-94739-6

Table of contents

Acknowledgements

No book is written alone. I am so grateful to the trailblazing healers who have gone before me, which made my journey easier. To my healer friends who make my life more joyful by helping me with my own physical and emotional healing, I thank you most of all. That includes Astara Livingston, Angie Montgomery, Angie Pennisi, Cara Lazure, Elari Onawa, Christina Pierce, Danielle Studnicka, Denise Schumacher, Frank Wolfe, Gabriele Kohleiber, Jenny Fullerton, Jill Schrack, Marina Gray, Marlene Porter, Michaela Mast, Orion Muff, Rebekah Lowe, and Rick Reynolds. I wish you all knew how much you have affected my life as well as the thousands of others whose lives you've touched just by being you and bringing your wonderful energy to this planet.

Introduction

Have you been having experiences you cannot explain? Maybe feeling the energy of a deceased loved one? Are you getting what you think are messages from deceased loved ones like pennies or cardinals or maybe even repeating numbers, but you wonder if you are crazy? Perhaps you are starting to know certain things before they happen? Or you just get a gut feeling about something? Trust me, you are not alone, which is why I wrote this book. What we, who live in the world of woo-woo, call the veil is the thinning of energy and experiences between the physical or 3D world and the spiritual realm or the astral plane.

More and more people are having these paranormal experiences and either do not know what to do with them or are having their interest piqued and wanting to learn more.

That is what this book is about: to educate and inform on a beginning level about the world beyond the physical realm where we, as humans, reside. There are so many pieces to the gigantic cosmic puzzle that it can be overwhelming. The following chapters help breakdown by modality how the spirit world can be contacted, listened to, and allowed to assist us in our human lives.

I began my spiritual journey at the age of 21 when I was introduced to the concept of past lives through a book recommended to me. I knew I was different from the time I was young. I knew I had interesting experiences but thought everyone else did too. What I did not realize was that I was a psychic medium in training, which is now my full-time occupation. Through the book, *The Search for Bridey Murphy*, I was introduced to a world that felt completely normal to me. The more I learned and studied, the more I was able to understand myself as well as the world around me and beyond me. That was more than 40 years ago. The more I learn, the more I realize what I do not know. How daunting is that?!

As you read this book, certain things might resonate with you and others might not. That is ok. Not everything is meant for you. Everything in this book is also from my own experiences, research, and input from my clients as well as other alternative practitioners. No one knows for sure what the spirit world is all about until they are on the other side of the veil. If anyone claims to have the answers, well, they are wrong! We can only form our opinions on what we have experienced or what truly resonates with our soul. The rest will be revealed to us when it is our time to leave our physical body and join the astral or spiritual plane. I will say that the journey to discover who you really are through the following chapters will be the most joyous journey you will ever take. It will not be easy, but life isn't easy either, is it? Why not make it a journey to help you discover who you really are and why you decided to inhabit a human body on the planet Earth? This book will not fully give you answers, but it will give you the tools to further explore yourself, to help you understand why you are here and provide alternative healing modalities.

I have spent decades working with most, but not all, of the modalities in the following chapters and can tell you from personal experience that they all have something amazing to offer if you are willing to commit to your own healing and understanding. After my mother passed away, I made a commitment to heal my physical body, my emotional body, and my spiritual body - no matter what it looked like. I have come a long way, but just when I think I have this thing called life all figured out, something from my past reaches out and whaps me in the face. When I say past, the past could be from a past life or my current life. This journey of healing and self-discovery never ends. As I continue the journey and discover new modalities, I find myself more and more excited about what lies ahead. I hope you discover the same – that getting to know yourself through alternative healing methods will be the most joyous journey that you ever take too!

I am not saying that you should ignore more traditional forms of healing. Going to your regular physical doctor or mental health practitioner is equally as important as going the alternative route. Remember when I said the commitment to myself was to heal no matter what it looked like? Well, for me, that includes traditional Western doctors as well as more Eastern alternative healers. They all have their place; and it is up to us to take charge of our own physical, spiritual, and emotional health and do what is best for our bodies, minds, and spirits.

The most important thing you can do is to listen to your own inner guidance. It will never fail you. There is a difference, however, in your ego and your inner guidance. Your ego will lie to you every time! Your inner guidance will never lie or fail you in any way. As a psychic medium, I work with my clients and help them on their journey. However, when it comes to my own journey of healing and abundance, I often rely on and go to other practitioners to ensure I follow what is best for me and not what my ego is telling me what is best for me.

This book is a wonderful place for you to start. It is divided into two parts. The first part is understanding the journey to **you** and the things that are happening to you or have grabbed your interest. The second part is talking about the actual alternative healing modalities. You can begin your journey by reading the following chapters and start tuning in to which of the modalities appeal to you and resonate with your soul. Those are the modalities you will want to research further. For now, what I have listed is the introduction to many of the alternative healing modalities existing today. Which ones excite you? Which ones pique your interest? This book gives you a place to start, a place to help explain what has been happening to you or to guide you in the journey of a lifetime. A journey to the other side of the veil. Enjoy and read in peace, light, and understanding.

Part One

"I believe that unarmed truth and unconditional love will have the final word in reality."

- MLK

The Veil is Thinning

In the past several years I have felt and seen that the veil is thinning between this world and the other side which we can call heaven or the astral plane. More and more people are contacting me with their own "strange" experiences. Of course, none of them are strange to me as I live my life every day with these so-called strange experiences. I do understand, however, that when you experience things for the first time, they can appear to feel strange. That is the main reason I am writing this book: to demystify the spirit world and explain what these strange things really are and mean. We are going to cover topics such as NDE (near death experiences), spirit guides, soul mates, reincarnation messages from the other side, and many more.

This book is to tell you that you are NOT crazy! Most of us have been taught or programmed to believe certain things such as "What you see is what is actually real" or "Messages from the other side are a sin and should not be toyed with." Others include "If you cannot prove it, it does not exist" or my favorite…"Here take this pill and it will all go away." We are so much more than what we can currently explain, more than our five senses and our physical bodies. We are multi-dimensional beings and are in the state of beginning to recognize that!

One of my favorite things is when a new client comes to me and says, "You're going to think I'm crazy, but…" Let me put your mind at ease – I never think anyone is crazy. Believe me, I have experienced enough crazy stuff on my own that I certainly will not think you are crazy!

Let me clarify – I am not a therapist. When someone comes to me with issues that I am not trained or equipped to handle, I will recommend a therapist since therapy is not my training or expertise. But I will tell you that those times are rare. Most people are just looking for clarification and guidance. That I can do!

Many times, when the veil begins to thin, people will experience things such as knowing who is calling as soon as the phone rings or thinking of someone who then suddenly reaches out. Isn't it cool when that happens? It is not scary, is it? It is actually fun!

Another thing that might happen is when a loved one dies, we might think we see them out of the corner of our eye but when we turn to look no one is there. We then make the leap to thinking we are crazy or that we just miss them so much that it is our imagination working overtime.

Every major religion in the world believes in life after death. However, many of them believe the deceased cannot be communicated with or that it is a sin to do so. Nothing could be further from the truth. After years of talking to deceased loved ones, I can tell you they only come through with messages of love. Yes, even those souls who were less than wonderful while they were here now have clarity and will deliver messages of love from the other side.

When they first appear to me, they will show me the energy they had while in human form which might include words or actions that were harmful. They only present themselves this way so my client and I will recognize that we have the right soul. After identity is established the energy changes completely. Your loved ones come through offering forgiveness, asking for forgiveness, but mostly, delivering messages of love. They want us to know that we have a huge team of spirits on the other side cheering us on in our quest to accomplish what we came here to accomplish and learn the lessons we came here to learn. This team includes not only deceased loved ones but also spirit guides, angels, and a council of elders. Did you know that? You have such a huge team to help and guide you through this difficult journey of life on Earth. Pay attention to them! Make them your best friends because, believe me, they are!

Please know that when you think you feel your deceased mother come through – it is her. Trust that, when you repeatedly see hawks in the sky and your mind goes to your grandfather, it is him telling you he is with you always. Deceased loved ones are sending us messages all the time. It is up to us to pay attention!

More than 15 years before my mother passed or was even ill, she came from Sioux Falls to Omaha to visit me. Out of the blue she told me the number 11:11 was "her" number. It meant something wonderful to her. When she said that, I walked over to my bookshelf and showed her the book *11:11* by Solara. We gave each other the look we all know, "Wasn't that a coincidence," although I knew it was no coincidence but did not realize what that number would eventually symbolize for me. When my mother eventually passed, I repeatedly started seeing 11:11 and 1:11. Spiritually it can mean something else, but to me I know it is my mother stopping by to say hello. Now more than 10 years after her passing, I still see 11:11 or 1:11 almost twice a day! I look at the heavens and say, "I love you, mom!" I want her to know I not only believe but I KNOW it is her. I am grateful every day for her message of numbers to me.

My father used to send cigarette smoke to me when he was sending me a message. Although I appreciated the affirmation, I've never liked the smell of cigarette smoke, so I asked him to change his way of communicating with me. Now, I no longer smell cigarette smoke – thank you, Dad! I usually only see his face or feel his presence when he wants me to know he is around. Additional common signs from the other side are pennies, cardinals, feathers, or hawks. I do not know why they choose those items, but they do! Others will send something very personal to remove any doubt it is them coming through for you. For instance, I was doing a reading for a woman when her grandfather came through. My client just nodded her head, acknowledging that she expected him to come through for her. Well, he did not disappoint! The next thing he showed me was a bowling pin, and I asked her what it meant to her. She reached down behind her and pulled out a miniature bowling pin attached to her key chain and said, "I was hoping he'd bring that up!" There was no second guessing that one! He came through loud and clear and left no doubt to his granddaughter that he was still with her.

Do you ever turn on the radio and hear a deceased loved one's favorite song? Or a song that reminds you of them? It is your loved one coming through and letting you know they are happy and in a good place. I had a friend pass away from cancer, and on the way to his funeral, I asked him if he was ok. I just needed a sign from him. He told me to turn on the radio, so I did. Guess what song was playing? *From a Distance*, sung by Bette Midler. Part of the lyrics are "God is watching us from a distance." It was the perfect song at the perfect time. My friend offered the best sign that he was still with me.

What "crazy" things have started to come through for you from your loved ones on the other side? Sometimes it can be as simple as you thinking you see something out of the corner of your eye but when you turn your head, nothing is there. Trust that someone is with you…and not in a scary ghostly kind of way. It is simply your loved one coming through to say hello and tell you they love you; they are happy and at peace.

You can talk to them too! They want to know that you recognize them. Many of us get in what I call receiving mode – we wait for them to contact us. Did you know you can talk to them anytime you choose? Ask them a question. Tell them you need a sign. Acknowledge them when you feel their presence. If possible, they love you even more from the other side than when they were here in human form.

Let us talk about precognition next. This goes beyond knowing who is on the phone before it rings. Precognition is the ability to just "know" things before they happen. This is happening more and more often to more and more people. When you have that feeling your child should not go out with friends on a particular night. When you feel weird about driving a particular route you take every day, so you change your course. Sometimes it can be called mother's intuition. Nobody questions mother's intuition; people love to hear those kinds of stories. This is precognition. It can and probably is happening to you, but you might be calling it a coincidence or just a fluke. Trust me, it is not. It is precognition beginning to work its magic in your life. Take it, learn from it, and ask for more. Spirit will always deliver!

When my spiritual and precognitive gifts were developing, I was getting information I did not necessarily want. I had the ability to know when people were going to die. That information would come rushing out of my mouth before I could stop it, which caused some extremely uncomfortable situations, let me tell you!

I finally realized that knowing when people were going to die really served no good purpose. No one needs to know that information, including me. I asked spirit to no longer give me negative information. I now ask for messages that are for my client's and my healing and highest good. Whew. I no longer get messages of death, thank goodness.

You have the same control. As the veil thins and people start getting messages from deceased loved ones or their spirit guides, they can go to that scary place. You know the place – where the mind goes down the rabbit hole and begins to imagine horrible situations. Do not go there! Set the perimeters up front with your guides. Tell them you do not want negative information unless there is something you can do about it. For instance, you get a message that your child will be in a car accident and seriously hurt. By all means, ask for that information if there is a way you can contact your child to prevent him/her from not getting in the car that day. That is not negative information but rather is helpful information. If there is something you can do about it – go for it. Receive those messages. If there is nothing you can do about it, why get the information ahead of time? It really serves no good purpose. Just know you can specify with your guides and loved ones the messages you want to receive and those you do not.

Doesn't that feel more empowering and less scary? Your guides are there for a reason: to make your life easier. They cannot interfere with your life plan, but they can certainly give you signs and messages to help make your path a bit easier. Your job is to pay attention. Listen to them. Watch for signs. They are there right in front of you every day. The more you pay attention, the more signs you will see. Ask for signs too. If you are confused about something, go ahead and ask! However, be patient when waiting for that sign. Sometimes signs will show up for you immediately. Other times it can take weeks, months, or even years. You must be ready to receive the signs when they come.

Instead of it being frightening when that veil begins to thin for you, please know that the universe is conspiring in your favor. Your job is to ask and then listen.

opening And closing intuition

As you begin to awaken on your spiritual journey, you will find it might be scary and confusing as well as joyful and peaceful.

Everyone is born with intuition. Some people come into their lives with fully developed psychic skills. Others are born with only a beginner's knowledge of their intuitive abilities. You can choose to develop those skills or not. There are so many places to go to learn if you choose to develop or enhance what you came into this life to learn.

I want you to know that you always have control! You can tell your guides as well as any spirit to "bring it on" or "back off." There is such a thing as universal law and spirit must listen and obey.

As you begin to experience things such as messages from loved ones on the other side or just a knowing of things about to happen, please understand that you are not nuts! These things are real. People might not believe you; they might be skeptical or even judgmental. That does not mean what is happening to you is not true. It is – trust it. I have always said that the people who question their sanity are usually the ones who are saner than the rest of us. Those who have mental health issues rarely question it.

As the veil between this world and the other side thins, an increasing number of people are having paranormal experiences. As more people are courageous enough to voice what is happening to them, the world is becoming more open minded and the paranormal is becoming more mainstream. Thank goodness! It is about time! Connecting to spirit is really a very natural state of being.

As you begin to open to the other side, it is especially important for you to know that you can control it. For some people, the opening is slow and gradual, relatively easy to handle. For others, the opening can be jarring. An accidental blow to the head or some other situation may tell the other side you are ready!

Getting to know your spirit guides is extremely important and should be one of the first things you do as you begin this joyous journey. They will listen to you, help you, and guide you to make things easier. Once you get to know your guides, they will help you control how often and how much information is downloaded to you at any given time. You can also find ways to turn on the information as well as turn it off. Trust me, you cannot be "on" all the time. It is exhausting. Your guides will help you determine the best way to say "yes" and to say, "done for the day, thank you."

I cannot tell you how many times I have had clients come to me stating they cannot sleep because spirit is waking them up trying to get messages through to them. I used to deal with the same situation. Spirits would show up in the middle of the night to give me messages for the clients I had scheduled the next day. I finally started saying before I went to sleep that only my spirit guides or deceased loved ones connected directly to me were allowed during the night. The interruptions stopped immediately.

I begin each day with a meditation that includes calling my guides by name and thanking them for letting me do the work I do, for always being with me, and for clear messages I may receive that day for my client's and my healing and highest good. It is my sign to my guides that I am ready to work. At the end of the day, I thank my guides and say session over, which is my sign for messages to stop.

Many times, at a party or any kind of social gathering when people find out that I am a psychic medium, they will ask what I see around them or if I have any messages for them. No! I do not! I tell them there is preparation, including a meditation, that I must do to be ready to receive messages. That will usually get people to change the subject. My guides know I need time off like everyone else. I need days off; I need vacations…just like you. The point is to be gentle but firm when people ask you for any kind of reading. You have control. Your spirit guides should be your best friends and will listen to you, respect your wishes, and work with you as you travel your spiritual journey.

On many television programs, there are psychics who do impromptu readings for people on the street. This is only for dramatic effect, which makes for good television. The people that are being surprised with a reading are most certainly not that surprised. There are cameras everywhere, and they must sign legal release forms before any reading can begin. However, the public does not see that side of the surprise.

As you develop your psychic abilities, I am asking you to NOT stop people on the street with messages from loved ones. To me it is an invasion of privacy – period. You also do not know if the person will be receptive to the messages. Perhaps they have religious reasons for not wanting to speak to the dead. Perhaps the loss has been so new that they are still in the grieving process. Perhaps they do not want to know or are non-believers. Your job is to read for those people asking for messages only whether it is a professional setting or simply for family and friends.

As you awaken, you can use the information you receive in any way you choose. You do not have to be a professional psychic medium. You can use your new gifts to help only yourself and your family. You can choose to say "No, not for me" and shut things down completely. The choice is yours – always yours. Please remember that if things get overwhelming, you can say "No," "Not right now," or "Slow it down just a bit." They WILL listen. You have control.

Protection

When inexperienced people begin having psychic experiences or are starting their spiritual path, they need to understand the importance of protecting themselves. I do not want to scare or frighten anyone; I simply want to education and inform. Protection is class 101 of the spiritual life.

Without protection, you are inviting any spirit to enter your consciousness no matter at what level they vibrate. Trust me, you do not want low vibrating spirits to influence you! They might be harmless pranksters, but they might also not have your best interest at heart. You want only spirits who have your healing and highest good as their intent.

When I do readings or Reiki with any of my clients, I invite in specific arch angels, deceased loved ones, angels, or guides who have messages for the client's healing and highest good, so no other spirit is allowed input. Many people have deceased loved ones who vibrate at a low level. They are definitely not welcome! So, whether you are playing with a Ouija board, tarot cards, runes, or merely tuning in to spirit, you want to set boundaries to protect yourself.

There are several reasons why you might be under what some call a psychic attack and just as many ways to protect yourself. Here are a few reasons why you might be under a psychic attack:

1. If you believe you are under a psychic attack – That is really the only way these things work: if you have been told you are under psychic attack and you choose to believe it.

2. Attacks from spirit – It is no secret that people who smoke a lot, drink heavily, or do drugs are much more susceptible to a psychic attack. Their defenses are down. A normal healthy person has a naturally strong aura that acts as a protector. Those who do not take care of themselves have a weakened aura and immune system, which allows "easy access" to low vibrating spirits. There is such a thing as universal law, which means **you are always in control**. If you are being influenced by such spirits, you simply need to state that you are aware of universal law and they need to leave you alone and go away! They must obey and will leave immediately.

3. Attacks from people – Low vibrating souls are not always on the other side. Many live among us and take great joy in jealousy, revenge, or sending harm to another person. They do this by casting spells. The good news is that, if this happens to you, the most you will probably feel is discomfort. If you keep a positive attitude, practice regular protection, and have good intentions in all that you do, you should never be affected by these dark, low vibrating people. Again, the only way to be susceptible to a spell is if you believe it.

Following are other ways to protect yourself:

   a.   **Crystals** – Crystals come from the Earth and have healing energy the Earth naturally holds. Each type of crystal has specific energy to help with certain situations. My favorites for warding off negative energy are black tourmaline, clear quartz, and rose quartz. Black tourmaline absorbs negative energy, rose quartz represents love, and clear quartz magnifies the energy of whatever stone is next to it. I grid my house and office with these three stones. By griding, I place the three stones in each corner of my house or office. I also place them on the outside perimeters of my house. It is a double whammy of goodness!

b. **Smudging** – Smudging is a process to purify or cleanse an area of negative energy through the use of sage. Most people buy sage in bundles. I personally prefer loose white sage as it smokes longer and, for me, is easier to work with. You simply put the sage in a fireproof dish, light the sage, and let it burn until the flame goes out and you have continuous smoke. Walk around your house using a feather to push the smoke in the direction you want it to go. Focus mostly on windows and doorways and especially any dark corners in the house. Low vibrating spirits love to hide. When you smudge, make sure you have a door or window open on each level of your house, so spirit has a way to exit instead of running around in circles! People often ask me how often they should smudge, which really varies. I smudge lightly about once a month, depending on how many visitors have entered my space. If I feel my energy is off or the energy of the house feels funky, I will smudge more often. It just depends on how your house feels to you. In addition to sage, you can also smudge an area using a mirrored surface by reflecting negative energy off that particular surface and sending it back to whence it came.

c.   **White Light** – Part of my daily meditation is to surround myself with white and golden light. By sitting quietly, closing my eyes and then taking a deep breath, the actual words I use are, "I encircle myself in the white and golden light of God's love and divine protection." I also find that, if I surround myself in white light before I go out in crowded spaces, it helps me cope with the sometimes overwhelming energy that comes from crowded places.

d.   **Mantras** – A mantra is something you repeat over and over to solidify what you are looking for or expecting. An example of a protective mantra might be, "Thank you for protecting me from any negative energies that are not for my healing and highest good." Repeat it several times all at once or make it a part of your daily routine.

e.   **Good Intentions** – To me, good intentions are everything in life, including a form of protection. No matter what you do in life, good intentions will always make things better or easier. They may not be perfect, but the outcome will be better than without good intentions.

f.   **Meditation** – I love to meditate! (Please see the chapter on meditation.) No, I do not wear a saffron robe and sit on a mountain top with my fingers forming mudras for hours on end, but I do meditate every day for about ten minutes as part of my morning routine. What meditation does for me is get me aligned and keep me aligned with the universe. When you are one with the universe, you are SO protected! I cannot even begin to explain all the benefits of meditation; protection is just one of them.

g.   **Prayer** – Prayer is another form of meditation. Encircling myself in white light is a form of prayer too. You can also go directly to God/Goddess and ask for protection. It is as simple as asking your best friend for help.

Whatever method(s) you choose for protection, just know it is an important part of your daily routine. We are exposed to so much negativity and low vibrating energies in our day to day lives that we need all the protection we can get! Think of it this way, the more protected you are the better able you are to assist others who might not be as aware.

Society of Fear

What saddens my heart probably more than anything is when I observe people living in fear. Most of us do, and our current society has designed it that way. As you begin to open to a new spiritual path, you might find people judging you, criticizing you, or even ghosting you. This can create a life of fear where you question your sanity or follow with what others are telling you without listening to or trusting your own instincts. Simply put – this is living in fear.

Living in fear begins at an incredibly early age, from the time we are born. Our parents, in an effort to keep us safe, warn us of impending danger if we do certain things, such as touching a hot stove or running across the street into oncoming traffic. These warnings have the spoken or unspoken message that you will get hurt or even die if you do these things. We even have the expression, "A fate worse than death," which certainly put the fear of life in most of us. We are afraid to live in case we might die. How crazy is that?! We are all going to die eventually, so why not live until that time comes? I believe that no one dies before their time or without their own permission. It might feel to us left behind that it is before someone's time, but I assure you it is their time to go. Now, I am not talking about being stupid. It certainly would not be smart to run out in traffic or touch a hot stove although many of us have done exactly those things and survived.

One of my favorite scare tactics as a young girl was when all the neighborhood kids would go to the community pool almost every day in the summer. We would pack a small lunch and ride our bikes to the pool to spend the entire day. Every day my mother would tell us that we had to sit for an hour after lunch and not go back into the pool for fear of getting cramps and dying from drowning. I believed that tale for years until a new friend came with us one day and told the rest of us it was an old wives' tale, and we would not get cramps and die if we did not wait an hour. I remember being in awe at her news and tested those boundaries that very day by only waiting 45 minutes before I was back in the pool. For a minute I thought I felt a cramp coming on and had a brief moment of panic until I realized it was probably all in my head. The next day I waited only 30 minutes before I was back in the pool. After that, it was a free for all! I barely finished my sandwich before I was back in the pool with no adverse cramping at all. I do remember asking my mother about it and she did confess that it might not be true, but it would not hurt to wait an hour…just in case. Of course, the just in case was just in case I developed cramps and died.

That lesson shifted a very strong paradigm in my consciousness, and I began questioning other scare tactics that had been instilled in me. I was always amazed at how so many people did not question these things. They blindly obeyed what they were taught in an act of self-preservation, or so they thought. Not only do people do what they have been told, taught, or programmed, but they do not even question it and instead pass on to others, including their own families.

I am not judging. However, I find it so remarkably interesting that people trust what they are told without investigating it themselves. I understand that we also live in a world where there is a tsunami of information and is really impossible to keep up, but we can certainly question some things. I do notice commercials and advertising probably the most. If you do not use a certain product, you are less than and are subjecting yourself to ridicule or even being shunned by society.

Do you really want to work harder when you can use this product that will make your life so much easier and give you so much more leisure time? Here is the thing: with everything in the world today that supposedly makes our lives so much easier and gives us so much more time to spend with the people we love, why isn't that happening? It's almost a badge of honor or makes us more important to be so busy. Even those of us who believe in self-care have really just added one more thing to our to-do list!

If we do not drive the right kind of car, have the right kind of house, raise children to be perfect human beings, wear the right clothes, get on the latest trends to show we are "with it" and on top of what is happening in the world. We have agreed on some level to let it matter what others think of us and judge us. It is just another way living in fear affects us negatively. To me, smart phones are the prime example of all this craziness. The pressure to be available 24 hours a day is huge now. Whether it be by phone, email, text, or messenger, we are expected to respond within minutes when we are contacted. The presumption is that, if you do not respond when I try to contact you, you will make me worry that something has happened to you... that you are dead somewhere and I cannot get to you. We have the world at our fingertips and yes, in many ways it has made our lives easier, but in just as many ways it has made our lives even more hectic with the expectation of always being available. Along with the fear that is projected on to us also comes the element of shame. Essentially, if you do not respond immediately, you really do not care about the person reaching out to you. You are too important to care about others who are trying to connect with you. Our sense of boundaries has completely disintegrated, brought on by fear and shame. People are exhausted. They are tired and want change but do not know how to make that change. They are at point A and want to get to point B but have no idea how to do it – how to even get started.

I understand. Really, I do. I spent a good portion of my life on the phone, on a computer, in an airplane, just doing my job. I was so high strung, waiting for the next piece of criticism to be dropped on me like a veil of shame or pointing out my ineptness. Then it was time to react; I would react either defensively or go on the attack. There was no in between. The seething inside would begin as I would go back to my desk or call a willing listener who would commiserate with me about how mistreated we all were.

Finally, in 2004 I had had enough. I quit my job and opened my own business. What I did not realize for nearly another decade was that no matter where I went or what I did, I brought that fear with me. Nothing had really changed except my job. I created a similar environment to my corporate world, only now I did not have the salary or the benefits! That brought on an entirely new level of fear. I was trapped and did not know how to get out of it – like many of you feel, I am sure. Whether it is about a job or a relationship or your finances or your health. The cycle of fear continues and will always continue until you begin to think differently and ACT differently. So how do you do that?

It is like any addiction; and believe me, fear is as big an addiction as alcohol, drugs, gambling, or pornography. We have been doing it for so long, we no longer even recognize the patterns we have created and bury our heads deeper and deeper into the sand and the land of denial. I can hear your excuses from here! But… everybody lives in fear. But…it works for me; I am simply fine. But…I have tried, and my family makes it too difficult. But…it is not that bad – I have it under control.

But…but…but…

Think about it, when an alcoholic is challenged to quit drinking, they usually must go to rehab to get them out of the environment and relationships they are used to. When they leave rehab, unless they stay away from toxic people and places, chances are 100% they will be drinking within a day or two. They must change the way they think about themselves, alcohol, and those whom which they associate. The same is true for you. When you want to escape the claws of living a life in fear, you need to do the same thing. You probably do not have to do it as drastically as a substance abuse addict, but the theory is the same.

In 2010, I made a commitment to only myself that I was going to heal no matter what it looked like. That meant physically, mentally, and emotionally (body, mind, and spirit). Every day and every situation that came up I took a step back and thought about my reaction. Did my reaction support the thing I wanted most? For me it was peace. Defining what peace looked like and felt like to me supported living a fearless existence. I did not consciously drop friendships, but my changing be-havior caused a few of them to drop away. We no lon-ger needed each other to complain to, which was the basis of that friendship. There were many setbacks, but I kept on going. In fact, I am still moving forward and have realized that this is a journey that will never end.

That is what I want you to realize too. Your journey is just beginning and will last the rest of your life. What it takes is a deep commitment – a long-term, lifetime commitment every day to be the next best version of yourself. It does get easier, and it also gets more fun!

Negative things will undoubtedly still happen to you; but when life deals out those hard lessons, you will now have stores of built-in resiliency to bounce back quicker than you used to and with unquestionable strength to carry on, knowing you deserve that happy joyful life you originally signed up for.

I equate this journey to programming a computer. We have had a lifetime of being programmed to fear people, things, and ourselves. We now need to understand that we have the power to reprogram ourselves in whatever way we choose. It took many years for the original programming to happen, and it will take many years for the new programming to take hold. Trust that it is working. Trust that you are headed in the right direction. Trust that no one truly has control over you but you. It takes time and tenacity, but you can do it! I believe in you.

This does not have to be a lonely road either. Begin friending people who do not live in fear or are on the path to not living in fear. They will keep you company, be your friends, mentors, guides, and teachers. You will learn from each other because, even during your reprogramming, you have so much to give, so much to offer. Only those on the same path will recognize that and cherish you for your strength. Like the alcoholic, you must change the scenery, which includes hanging out at the same places and listening to the same people whine, complain, and judge but continue to stay stuck and wonder why. You must start your brave journey by first recognizing that you live in fear, have been programmed to live in fear, and no longer want to live in fear. Only then will you begin to recognize the pull society, friends, and family have over you. I know you love them, but separate yourself from them if you need to. Begin to claim the person you want to be and then take action to get there.

That is another key point to make. You must act! Everything you do must support the person you want to be, the life you want to live, the life of living fearlessly. Give it time, give it patience, give it relentless pursuit, but most of all, give it your best – even if your best is just crawling out of bed some days. Some days that is all we have – still, it is a move in the right direction.

Heaven And Hell

Heaven and Hell – well now, that is a subject worth investigating! Depending on the way you were raised, your religion, and how your beliefs might have changed through the years, everyone still has pretty strong opinions regarding heaven and hell.

Here are my opinions, which I have arrived at by talking to deceased souls on the other side and through my own personal experiences. Does Heaven exist? Yes! Does Hell exist? Yes! I enthusiastically answer these questions, but both answers come with a caveat. Yes, both Heaven and Hell exist but not in the way most people think. Let us start with Hell.

In conversations with those on the other side, Hell actually exists here on Earth. There is no "burning in Hell forever" kind of place. We come to Earth to learn lessons; and believe me, we pick some doozies. Those lessons can feel like Hell. The way people treat other people has always felt a bit like Hell to me.

I am always surprised when I have family members who book sessions with me to connect with their loved ones who have passed away, and they come with very interesting questions regarding the lifestyle of the person who passed. One of the most frequently asked questions is about loved ones who were of the LGBTQ community (lesbian, gay, bisexual, transgender, and queer). It makes me sad that people are so judgmental, especially with supposed loved ones. They will ask me if their gay loved one is in Hell. I emphatically answer, "NO!" I explain that many times their life here on Earth was Hell due to the way they were treated and abused by others. Their loved one is now in Heaven along with everybody else. They are at peace and reviewing their life to see if they accomplished what they came to Earth to accomplish – just like everybody else. They are loved unconditionally by the creator – just like everybody else.

I also get questions about people who lived lives of drug abuse, alcoholism, or any other addictive lifestyle. The same holds true. Their Hell was here on Earth. We do not know what lessons they came here to learn, so we have no right to judge. Maybe their lesson was to live a life of addiction. If so, they did it beautifully. Maybe their lesson was to live a life of addiction and to find the strength to recover. If they did not achieve it, they still go to heaven when they die and will have to come back to Earth and give it another try until they learn the lesson – the lesson they chose to learn – not a lesson passed on through religious teaching or anyone else's opinion.

So, let us move on to Heaven. Just like Hell, Heaven exists here on Earth too! Look around you at the trees, birds, beaches, mountains, cats, dogs, the sky. Listen to the sounds of water lapping on lakeshore, the wind through the leaves, children laughing in the distance. Smell the coffee brewing, bacon frying, your grandmother's perfume that makes you feel safe and loved, fresh rain on a spring day. Feel the skin of your partner, the softness of towels from the dryer, the dirt from your garden as you plant for another season, the sand on your feet as you walk on the beach. All these things are pieces of Heaven sent for you to enjoy. Do you enjoy them? Are you taking the time to enjoy them as a gift sent especially for you?

Heaven really does exist on the other side too. So many people wonder how it can exist when those who have had near-death experiences come back with some similar but also some quite different stories to report. For example, why does someone who is Jewish experience teachings from their religious upbringing while

Christians meet Jesus or God, and Muslims meet Allah? How can that be? Let us go back to the belief that if we are all one and we all come from source. Source can present itself as God, Jesus, Allah, or any other deity many of us have worshiped here on Earth while in human form. When we transition and get to Heaven, it is my understanding that we will see what we expect to see or what we have been taught to expect. The only exception is if people have been taught or threatened with eternal damnation. They most certainly will not find that!

What about people who claim to be agnostic or atheists? Are they going to end up in Hell as many religious zealots claim? The easy answer is NO. They will end up in Heaven with the rest of their religious relatives. If we believe that we are all one, then when someone dies and returns to source, it does not matter whether, in human form, they believed in God. Just because you do not believe in something does not mean it is non-existent. Maybe that is the very thing you wanted to experience in this lifetime, to be a non-believer. Believe me, there are plenty of people who claim to be believers in God and Jesus and follow the Bible religiously but judge and condemn their fellow man as well as do unconscionable things in their life. Have they earned the right to go to Heaven just because they "believed?"

No one earns the right to go to Heaven. That is where we came from and where we will return whether we were considered good people, bad people, believers, non-believers, or those who questioned it all.

Heaven is nothing but love. After all, love is the only thing that truly exists. Pure and unconditional love. As souls, that is what we are too – pure and unconditional love. The energy of pure and unconditional love.

When spirits visit me from the other side, they are always joyful. They typically will show up with their human personality and traits so I can identify them to my client. Once I have discussed their human personality, they almost always shift into what they are doing in Heaven. Trust me, not one spirit has shown up to me floating on a cloud with a bunch of cherubs playing harps. I have been told that some are teachers, some are students, some greet those who are in the process of transitioning from human to spirit. I have even had families show up together playing cards, dancing, and having a great time enjoying each other's company. Yes, even if they did not get along when they were in human form, they certainly get along in spirit form.

An exception is when a spirit comes through who was abusive or self-destructive when they were in human form. They do not necessarily show love, but they do come through asking for forgiveness. At the very least, they come through clarifying why they behaved the way they did. They are working on their soul growth and why they possibly did not learn the lessons they came here to learn. Earth is a big school and not an easy one. I have been told countless times that Earth is the densest planet in existence. It is also the hardest planet on which to live and learn. We all choose to continue to return to Earth until we have learned all the lessons and accomplish all that we came here to accomplish. Why do we continue to do this if it is so hard? It is one of the best ways for our souls to evolve.

That does not mean we cannot communicate from Heaven. When a spirit comes through from Heaven with apologies for a loved one, it is for their own soul growth, but it is also to relieve some pain or offer clarity to their loved ones still on Earth. It is so the ones still living can more easily learn and accomplish what they still have left to learn before it is their time to transition.

Heaven is a place of peace, joy, and unconditional love. That is it – period. There is no cause to fear death or judgment. No, you will not be bored floating around on clouds all day. There is still work to do. By work, I mean the main purpose of the soul is to evolve. The soul can evolve by doing work on Earth and in Heaven. They are both filled with lessons; it is just that the Earth lessons are harder because only on Earth do we get to experience hate, jealousy, anger, and sadness and because we forget who we are as souls when we enter the human body. In Heaven we still work, but we are truly clear about who we are and what we are to do to help souls evolve.

Meditation

Meditation is one of the most important things you will ever do for yourself. I can hear many of you saying, "I tried! I can't do that!" I am here to tell you that meditation can work for you.

There are a hundred plus different ways to meditate. With the drive-up window mentality our society has impressed upon us, we think we need to do things perfectly from the beginning and then have instant results too. That is not the case in most things.

People are also often of the mindset that you need to be wrapped in saffron robes and sitting on a mountain top to have a quality meditation. Not true unless you are a Buddhist monk or in training to be one.

The best way to begin meditation is to start and not give up! Like exercise, jogging is not the answer to everyone's exercise needs and neither is gymnastics, bike riding, swimming, or yoga. You must continue trying until you find what works for you. Also, just like exercise, you do not begin by running a marathon. You begin by walking, then walking further. You might then step it up to jogging a mile, then two miles until you reach your marathon goal of 26.219 miles. Even regular marathon runners still train before an event.

The same is true for meditation. Meditation is a practice where an individual uses a technique – such as mindfulness, or focusing the mind on a particular object, thought, or activity – to train attention and awareness and achieve a mentally clear and emotionally calm and stable state.

Think about it. Do you garden? Do you wash dishes by hand? Do you walk or run? These are all activities that can produce meditation! I like to think about meditation as any activity where you lose time. What that means is an activity where it is so automatic that your mind can wander elsewhere and not focus on the task at hand. You do not even have to train for it – most of us have some household activity that we do on a regular basis where we do not really have to focus. We just let our mind wander. That is one effective way to begin meditating!

When I was first attempting to meditate, I did what all the books told me to do – stare into a candle, stare in the mirror, get in the lotus position with my hands open or feet flat on the ground, and empty my mind. I do not know about you, but all those techniques, although they might work for some people, most certainly did not work for me. Empty my mind? You have got to be kidding! Next, I tried lying down on the bed right after I woke in the morning since I knew I would not be sleepy then and could focus on not focusing. Wrong! I just fell right back to sleep.

What I found that really worked for me in the beginning was to sit in a comfortable chair, feet flat on the ground and my hands placed wherever was comfortable that day. I began by taking a deep breath – in through my nose and out my mouth. I pictured the breath coming in the top of my head and out the bottom of my feet. Then I began each breath, picturing the color of each chakra. I began with red, representing the root chakra, breathing that color through the top of my head and out the bottom of my feet. In the beginning, at least 100 times per breath my mind interrupted me with things like, "Oh, I have to go to the grocery store" or "Oops, did I turn off the coffee pot?" The thing is, I always had somewhere to direct my mind off the chores and random thoughts and back to the color of each chakra (Chakras will be discussed in a later chapter).

The meditation would go something like this:

Deep breath

Now breathing in the color red through the top of my – what are all my appointments like today? – darn! Back to red coming through the top of my head, representing the root chakra located at the base of the spine. Now passing through my body and out the bottom of my feet – did I return that call to my sister? Oh wait, did I finish breathing out the bottom of my feet? Ok, back to it – red light going out the bottom of my feet. Well, that only took six different tries!

On to orange, representing the sacral chakra located below the belly button. In the top of my head – what should I cook for dinner tonight? Ok, starting over – in the top of my head, passing the orange breath through my body – maybe tacos would be good. The orange light is passing through my body – man, I hate laundry. I cannot believe it is laundry day again. The orange light continues to pass through my body and out the bottom of my feet.

On to yellow, representing the solar plexus located above the belly button, green for the heart chakra located in the middle of the chest, blue for the throat chakra located behind the throat, indigo for the third eye located between the brows, and purple for the crown chakra located at the top of the head.

Can you see that no matter how often the mind wanders or in what direction it decided to head, you have a place to redirect it. You CAN control your mind, but you are LEARNING to do it step by step and bit by bit. Also, know you will have good days and bad days. Some days will be a piece of cake to get through your meditation. Other days will take twice as long as your mind has a mind of its own and wanders endlessly. Once you have mastered the breath using your chakra colors – and believe me, this might take months or even years to master – you can begin adding things to your meditation, always giving your mind something to come back to as it goes off on its own little tangent.

Here are some other tools to use as you begin this beautiful journey: chanting, guided meditations (there are free guided sessions on YouTube), and background music (soft music will often eliminate background noise).

There are six other popular types of meditation:

1. Mindfulness meditation
2. Spiritual meditation
3. Focused meditation
4. Movement meditation
5. Mantra meditation
6. Transcendental meditation

What type is right for you? Whatever you choose, be kind to yourself. Give your mind something to go back to. Give yourself time to adjust to this new way of being. Think of beginning meditation as being in kindergarten. Would you chastise a 5-year-old for not being perfect? For not getting it right the first time? No, you would not. You would be gentle and guide them repeatedly until they started to get it on their own. Treat yourself like the child or beginner you are. Be gentle, be patient, be persistent. Meditation can bring amazing results if you stick with it and do not give up!

Some of the benefits of meditation can be:

1. Lower blood pressure
2. Reduced anxiety
3. Decreased pain both mentally and physically

Whether the benefits are scientifically proven or have the placebo effect, anyone who practices meditation will tell you the benefits they have realized.

So, let us look again at the different types of meditation and how they are different from each other.

1. Mindfulness Meditation

This is the most popular form of meditation used in the West. With mindfulness meditation, you pay attention to the thoughts as they pass through your mind. You do not judge these thoughts! Observe them as they pass through. You might look for repeating patterns. My definition of mindfulness is *Why do I think what I think and do what I do without judgment of myself or anyone else.* The next question to yourself is… does this continue to serve me? If not, let it go. If the answer is yes, hang on to it for now because you have made a conscious decision.

This is a great meditation to practice alone since you do not need a teacher to get started and make it part of your daily routine.

2. Spiritual Meditation

Spiritual meditation is similar to prayer in that you connect with the silence around you and connect to God on a deeper level. This can be practiced at home, in a place of worship, or outdoors. Personally, I love this form of meditation when I am at a beach and can feel the wonder of the universe with the wind blowing through my hair, the salty smell of the ocean, and the indentation as the sand moves beneath my feet. This form of meditation, for me, comes with nothing but gratitude.

3. **Focused Meditation**

Focused meditation involves concentration using any of the five senses. You might want to stare into a candle flame, listen to a gong or chimes, or count prayer beads. This form of meditation can be quite challenging and might not be for beginners. I remember when I was first attempting meditation, I tried this method and gave up pretty quickly. I tried the candle flame first and my thoughts were everywhere but on that flame! The thing is I did not give up. I just kept trying new ways until I found something that worked for me. After meditating for so many years, I now love to try different methods to mix it up a bit and see if new insights come through for me.

4. **Movement Meditation**

This is the meditation I mentioned earlier and can involve gardening, walking on the beach, doing the dishes, yoga, or any form of movement. This form of meditation is especially great for people who like to move and cannot sit still! Do the movement you love and let your mind wander to where it wants to go. Trust me, you will get amazing insight if you just allow it to come through.

5. **Mantra Meditation**

This form of meditation involves repeating certain words or phrases and is extremely popular in Eastern religions. There are CDs you can order online or purchase in your local metaphysical bookstore to help you get started. You can find mantras that focus on health, wealth, inner peace, etc. This is a great form of meditation for people who are uncomfortable with silence because it helps focus on the word(s) rather than the breath.

6. Transcendental Meditation

This form was immensely popular in the 1970s and was most referred to as TM. It is also the most popular form of meditation used around the world. This form can be created specifically for each person using a word or combination of words that will be most useful to the individual. This form is for those who have a serious commitment to meditation. It can also be a form to "graduate" to once you have become very comfortable with any of the other methods.

We all know it takes 21 days to make or break a habit. So, make a commitment to yourself that you will sit in meditation for a minimum of 5 minutes per day for 21 days. Pay attention to how you feel after each day. This is not meant to be forced but rather to be a commitment to your own personal growth and healing. Who does not want to do that?!

In the beginning of my meditation practice, I remember distinctly a morning where I was lying on my bed trying to focus on my breath. I hit that moment of letting go on a level I had never done before and was transported to a past life. The vision began by looking like the screen of an old black and white television set in my head. As the signal started to come in clearer, I saw myself as a man in the old West (and not a nice man!). I saw this man, as myself, heading into an old West town, getting down off my horse and tying the horse to a fence in front of a store or saloon. The energy I felt from this man, myself, was not healthy but full of pain and anger. I knew this man for he was me. I was going to start trouble wherever I went to reduce the pain and anger felt inside myself.

When I felt that painful, angry energy, I startled myself out of meditation. Afterwards, I felt shaken for the rest of the day. What I finally came to realize is that I had, what I like to call, a past-life hangover. I had some anger issues in my current life, and it turns out, I brought that angry energy with me from my past life. Once that was realized, I was able to let the angry energy go. Even though I was shaken by the experience at the time, I am now so grateful for it as it began my road to inner peace.

self-Discovery

The most important thing you will ever accomplish in your life is to be authentically you! The problem is that we have been programmed otherwise from the time we are born. If you stop crying, you will get fed. If you behave in the store, I will buy you something. If you are good, I will give you a cookie. We learn to say yes to other people's demands and behave in a certain way before we are even aware that we are individuals. We get so used to saying yes to appease other people, we forget who we are along the way. At some point in our lives, we stop and wonder why we are not happy. I often hear people say, "I have everything I ever wanted. Why am I not happy?" Sometimes I will hear something different. "I keep searching and searching but can't find the answers."

The reason people are not happy or cannot find the answers is because they have lost sight of who they are, who they are meant to be, and why they are here. They never stood a chance with parents, friends, siblings, teachers, and co-workers all telling them what to do, how to behave, and what is expected for them to "win" approval from people outside of themselves and, therefore, be good enough. My questions to you are, "Good enough for whom? Good enough for what?"

If you ever want to be happy, simply ask yourself three questions.

1. Who am I?
2. What do I want?
3. What does that feel like and look like to me?

When I ask clients these questions, I usually get the "deer in the headlights" look. They are typically surprised they do not know the answers to these very simple questions. They ARE very simple questions but not necessarily with simple answers. There is a reason so many people are on anti-depressants. Actually, there are many reasons, but I believe lack of self-awareness and self-worth could be the major reasons. Let us look at each question again with greater detail.

Who Am I? One of the first things you need to do on the path to discovering you is to ask yourself the question "Who am I?" I want you to make a list of at least 25 adjectives that describe you. You cannot use labels such as wife, husband, son, daughter. You must use words such as dependable, loyal, funny, stuck, searching. Preferably, the words are all positive in nature, but if they are not, that is ok too! As an example, one woman I was working with showed me her list of 25 words describing herself. One of the words was clumsy. I challenged her on that word. As a psychic medium, when I heard that word on her list, I immediately got a psychic "hit." I told her that when she was three someone told her she was clumsy, and she chose to believe it. She has spent the rest of her life believing it and trying to make that statement true. Once she became aware of that word and how it came into her consciousness, she could let it go because it really was not true, and it no longer served her. She could then replace the word clumsy with something else that would now serve her in a better way.

Making a list of 25 words describing yourself will be one of the most powerful things you will ever do. You can do this in one sitting, or it might take days, weeks or even months to complete. There is no deadline! Once the list is complete and you really look at it, you will realize what a powerful human being you are! You just never took the time to define it. Now you have! The first time I made my list I emailed three people to assist: a family member, a close friend, and an acquaintance. I told them I was working on a project and needed their help and then asked them to describe me in three words. When I received answers, most of the words were already on my list, but there were two words that I had not even thought of and yet they were correct. It was so enlightening to get input on how others saw me and how that differed in alignment with how I saw myself.

This project will define who you are – who you REALLY are. I was shocked when I looked at my list. Some of my first thoughts were, "Who wouldn't hire this person?" "Who wouldn't fall in love with this person?" "Who wouldn't want to hang with this person?" I was so surprised, but with even more scrutiny, I realized the words I had written down were true. That project completely changed my perception of myself. It will change the perception of yourself too! It is the first step in learning how to love yourself. If there are less than positive words in your list, do not focus on them in any other way than to decide how you would like those words to change. As a society, we tend to focus on the negative. Please do not do that! Focus on the positive things that are uniquely you.

What Do I Want? This question is a bit more difficult. We spend our early years acquiring things. I want a new toy. I want a car. I want a house. I want new furniture. I want a new job. If you look closely, all of these "wants" are external things. Just things. What we really want is never the house, the car, or the job. What we genuinely want is, what I call, a base emotion. We want balance, peace, happiness, security, freedom, love, joy. For now, just pick one of those words that might have resonated with you. My word is peace.

I was talking to a friend of mine one day when I asked her what she wanted out of life. She said all she wanted was to be organized. With a smile, I told her that was not what she really wanted. She gave me a look of confusion laced with a bit of contempt. How dare I correct her on what she wanted! I then asked her how she would feel if she was organized. She answered, I would feel happy. That is what she really wanted in her life – to be happy. Getting organized was just one step in getting her to her ultimate goal – happiness.

Look at your life. Is it balanced? Are you happy? Are you at peace? Do you feel safe and secure? Do you feel free to be yourself? Do you feel loved? All these words might resonate with you, but for now, just pick one. You can change this word whenever you feel the need – after all it is your word. In fact, twice a year I go through all three questions to review and update. I think this is so important to remain clear about who we are and what we want. After all, things change constantly; we change constantly. The person who does this exercise this year and actually does the work, will find that they will undoubtedly be a completely different person 2 or 3 years from now. As you get to know yourself and realize what a wonderful journey it is, your standards for yourself will keep going higher and higher. You will soon realize that anything is attainable, but you must realize exactly what it is that want to attain.

Many years ago, I was having lunch with a friend. I was whining that I just wanted peace in my life…really, all I wanted was a little peace. He asked what peace looked like to me. I just stared wide-eyed at him, not having a clue how to answer that question. His next question was, "How can you have peace in your life if you don't know what it looks like?" We changed the subject, finished our lunch, and left. However, I could not shake the question he had asked," What does peace look like to you?" Later that day I wrote down my answer in only four or five sentences and became truly clear on what peace looked like and felt like to me. It took a few years, but I now have peace in my life every single day. All it took was a few minutes to clarify what I wanted and what it looked like and felt like, and now I have it in my life constantly. That is a miracle, don't you think? So, what is peace to me? I know in life we are here to learn lessons, experience moments, and accomplish things. I also know that no one gets through life unscathed; life beats the stuffing out of all of us. So, my definition of peace was not to learn the lessons, not to experience or accomplish. I knew I still had to and wanted to do those things. What I wanted was to have peace in my head no matter what was happening around or outside of myself.

That brings us to the third question:

What does what I want look like and feel like to me? Do you want peace like I did? Do you want freedom? Security? Love? Balance? Happiness? Joy? Take a few minutes now and write a description of what you want and what that looks like and feels like to you. I really recommend that you do these exercises on your own. The reason I say that is because a few years ago I was working with a client on this very thing. She concluded that peace was her word just as it was mine. At this point, she had no idea that peace was my word too. I asked her to define what peace felt like to her. Her answer? "My five dogs laying all over me." I told her that sounded like hell to me. Do not get me wrong, I love animals. I just do not want five dogs on top of me! We laughed, and I told her my word was peace, too. Isn't it amazing that two people can have the same word with completely different meanings?

That is why I want you to do this exercise alone. You and your spouse, partner, child, friend, parent could end up with exactly the same word, but chances are you will have completely different definitions.

After you have decided on your word and you have

clarified it to yourself and the universe, I now want you to wear your word over your head like a banner.

Everywhere you go, whatever you do – remember your word. With every decision you make, ask yourself the question, Does this support peace in my life? Does this support freedom in my life? Does this support balance in my life? Or whatever word you have chosen. Does this support the person I want to be in my life? Does this support the kind of life I want to live? Can you see how this narrows the decision-making field for you? It eliminates all the white noise of others having their input and, therefore, confusing you with your true goals. In other words, it helps you keep your eye on the ball, on what is now your priority.

When I first claimed peace as my word, I would constantly ask myself that question. Does having constant financial stress in my life support peace? No! After a few months of emphatically answering that question regarding the business I then owned, I put the business up for sale. Did that decision support peace in my life? Well, the jury was still out on that one, but at least I knew I was not stuck. I could move in the direction of possible peace. Staying where I was, I was assured more of the same. I am not saying this is an easy journey. It can be incredibly difficult, but at least you are moving in the right direction. The more you move in the right direction, the more success you will have and then the more success you will want. This is the pathway to discovering you! Claiming you! Living your best life!

Sure, there will be disappointments along the way. Yes, there might be failures. There might be steps that feel like you are moving backwards. I promise you that you are not! You are refining and tweaking what you want and making it clearer to yourself and the universe. You see, the universe wants you to have what you want

– you ultimately must be clear about it. What you are doing is giving the universe permission to send these wonderful things to you.

When defining what you want, however, you need to create a template, not too detailed, and in doing so, the universe will give you something better than you could have ever dreamed of yourself! Your job is clarity and allowing the universe to do its job. There might be certain things that perfectly fit the framework of what you said you wanted, but when it shows up for you, it just does not feel right. You have the right to say no! You can say to the universe, "Thank you but let us tweak this opportunity just a bit, ok?" Step back and let the universe work its magic! So, how do you build a template? What is a template? To me, a template is a different way of manifesting. So how do you manifest?

Manifesting

To me, manifesting is creating a template of what you want in your life. I work with many people who come to me looking for love in their life, in particular, romantic relationships. Don't all of us want love in our lives? I do! But many of us are not clear as to what that looks like. I was talking to a friend of mine several years ago who wanted to get married and have children. I asked her what she was looking for in a relationship and she told me 1) he must be at least 6'1", 2) he must have brown hair, and 3) he must make at least $100,000 per year. Wow. I asked her, "Does he have to be nice?" She looked at me like I just flew in from outer space. "Of course, he has to be nice," she said to me with a look of wonderment on her face. I wondered why that was not first on her list instead of how tall he needed to be. She did end up meeting, marrying, and having children with a genuinely nice man, I am happy to say. But what if she did meet a man who fit her criteria but who treated her badly? She got what she asked for and was lucky enough to get the important things too. You can manifest whatever you like, but to me, it is more meaningful to manifest world peace, love, and light rather than a piece of jewelry. Make sure your needs are being met and then move on to manifesting more global things.

Whether you are manifesting love in your life, a new job, a new home, or a new life, the formula is the same! First, you always begin with gratitude. Gratitude will turn your life upside down. I always ask clients," What's the first thing you say when someone gives you something?" Most people answer automatically, "Thank you!" Good answer! When you begin with thank you, you act as if you already have it.

Therefore, you begin your template with:

Thank you for the perfect person for me.

Thank you that he/she is emotionally healthy.

Thank you that he/she is spiritually healthy.

Thank you that he/she is physically healthy.

Thank you that he/she is financially healthy.

Thank you that he/she loves and supports me in all that I do.

Can you see how this is a template for what you want? This is not detailed to the point of height, weight, and income because that truly does not, or at least should not, matter. What does matter is that your emotional needs are met. The rest is just detail that we leave up to the universe.

Next pay attention to how you feel when you have the perfect mate. How does your head, heart, and body feel? True manifesting is sitting in the emotion of what you are creating, acting as if you already have what you want and need.

When I first decided to go public as a psychic medium, I needed office space. I already agreed to share space with a healer friend of mine, but her current lease would not be up for about 4-6 months, which meant I needed space for 4-6 months. How in the world was I going to find that?!

I used my trusty template and came up with this:

Thank you for the perfect office space for me.

Thank you that the rent is no more than $250 a month.

Thank you that there will be no lease.

Thank you that I will be welcome for 4-6 months.

Thank you that it is in the perfect location for me.

Thank you that it is available immediately.

Guess what happened? The next day I received a text on my phone. It was from someone who messaged apologies to me for taking so long to get back to me. She had written down my phone number wrong and mixed up two of the numbers, and did I still want to look at the place? Huh? I did not even remember contacting this person but still agreed to look at the space.

She gave me the address and I almost dropped the phone. It was in the exact part of town where I wanted to be. It was in a secure building and in a wing of the building that housed all alternative healers! The lady renting the space had already rented a three-office suite and was looking for two other alternative healers to lease the open two offices.

I told her I would only need the space for 4-6 months. She told me that was perfect. I asked about a lease, and she said there was no lease; it was a gentleman's agreement of sorts. I could move in immediately and decorate however I chose. Wow. Now, on to the last question...how much is the rent? $250.00 a month. You have got to be kidding me!

I gave the universe a big thank you and moved in the next day. I stayed in that location for 5 months until my friend and I were ready to move into our new location. It was the perfect spot at the perfect time with the perfect person. That is how manifesting works! It can work for you too!

I have manifested two cars, two office spaces (I am still at the second location), and 2 homes among countless other things, not to mention peace in my life as I mentioned earlier.

When people are skeptical of manifesting, I show them how to start with the simple stuff – the perfect parking place at the grocery store. Anyone can do that! For many people, the perfect spot is next to the entrance. For me, it is next to cart return. I like to walk, so I do not care about being close to the entrance. What I do care about is, that after I have loaded groceries in my car, I can put the cart back where it belongs, jump in my car, and leave. It works every time! So, if manifesting is new to you, try starting with something like the perfect parking place.

Here is what I find interesting – so many people have fun manifesting the small stuff. They get stuck when they perceive things to be big or hard. The small stuff is a piece of cake, but big things must surely be difficult, right? Wrong! Manifesting is manifesting! Everything already exists, and now it is simply up to you to claim it. Be clear as to what you want and that you really DO want it. So many people find themselves to be undeserving. Why? Most of the time it is the way we were raised. Our parents usually have the best of intentions for us, but sometimes that can backfire in unsuspecting ways.

I tell people I was raised to walk the tightrope of mediocrity. I could not fail, or I would embarrass the family. I also could not succeed too much, or I would be above the way I was raised and end up conceited, with a big head, or arrogant in some way. I am here to tell you that is ridiculous! It has been my experience that arrogant, conceited people are the most insecure. Those who are confident in themselves are generous and kind. Who do you want to be around?!

It took me years to make sense of the way I was raised. I understand my parents were trying to protect me from a harsh world and did the best they could. I also understand that, on a soul level, I picked them to be my parents so they could assist me in living out my life plan. In my world, there is no blaming anyone but ourselves because we picked our parents, siblings, our life plan. So, what is a life plan? We will get to that in another chapter, but, for now, let us get back to manifesting.

To me, the trick of manifesting is to be very clear in what you want. I mean clear on a soul level, not necessarily on a conscious level. Here is an example: Before I went public as a psychic medium, I owned a small art school. After eleven years I was ready to sell the business and move on to something else. What that something was, I did not know. What I did know is that I had about a year's worth of money before I needed to get a job. I decided I was going to make a very conscious choice about my next career and not just go for any kind of job. I took out my resume and asked the question, "Where was I the happiest?" I checked off each job with a resounding "NO!" In frustration, I threw my resume up in the air and out loud said, "Too bad I can't make a living at metaphysics. It's been the one and only constant in my life." You see, on a conscious level, I did not believe I could make a living as a psychic medium; but evidently, on a soul level, I did believe it because here is what happened next.

Two days after that declaration, I went to a Reiki practice session. I was practicing my Level II skills before I went for the Master Level. That night only the teacher and I showed up for practice, which had never happened before. The teacher told me I would have to practice on her. I just laughed and told her that doing Reiki on her was like doing Reiki on puppies and rainbows since her energy was always so good.

The minute I put my hands on her I knew something was very wrong. With every new hand position, I began to get sicker and sicker until I finally had to stop out of fear of fainting or throwing up. My teacher finally told me what was going on. Her mother had recently passed away, and she could feel her around her. She also said we could stop if I did not feel well. What? Suddenly I felt fine. I realized I was paying so much attention to placing my hands in the correct Reiki positions that I was not paying attention to the fact that her mother was trying to get my attention. At that moment, I put the proverbial stick in the ground and claimed the fact that I was a psychic medium. My teacher's need for closure with her mother was greater than my fear of failing or of being "found out" that I indeed was a psychic medium. That night I gave my teacher a spontaneous reading and thought no more about it. My teacher was a safe person who I knew would never ridicule me like so many others had done in the past when unedited things would come flying out of my mouth. I left that night grateful that I could help in some small way.

Not more than two days later my phone began ringing with people asking me if I was a psychic medium. What?! My "safe" teacher not only did not ridicule me, but she was referring people to me! At that point I said, "Yes." I shudder now to think where I would be if I had said, "No." But yes, is what I said and then began my career as a psychic medium. By listening to my soul, I also gave myself permission to dream.

Of course, it was not a full-time business in the beginning; so, to take away some financial pressure, I decided to find a part time job to supplement my income while I built my business. Can you guess what happened next? I overheard a conversation where someone said a particular company in Omaha, where I live, was looking to hire a stylist on a part-time, on-call basis. I could hardly believe it. I immediately applied for the position online and was hired within a few weeks. For those of you not familiar with an on-call position, it basically means that if the company does not need you on a particular day, week, or month, you do not work. In addition, if you cannot work for a particular day, week, or month, you do not go in. For example, if I had a client who could only come and see me on a Monday at 10AM, I could tell my boss I was unavailable to work until noon on that Monday. In other words, it was the perfect job for me while I built my business. In two years, I was able to resign from that position and go full time as a psychic medium. It was the perfect job at the perfect time for both the company and me.

Do you see how powerful manifesting can be? On a conscious level, I did not believe I could do it. On a soul level, I did believe it; and the universe handed me the perfect circumstances to make that happen. Creating templates can clarify what you want and allow you to trust the universe will give you something greater than you could have ever imagined. With too much detail, the universe will give you exactly what you ask for. Using a template, the universe will give more than you could ever imagine or dream!

Remembering Who You Are

We all know exactly who we are when we are in spirit form before we decide to come to Earth in human form. We have plans, plans for lessons we want to learn, things we want to experience, and goals we want to accomplish when we live this human life. We have agreements with our soul group of how we are going to interact with, learn from, and teach each other. In other words, we incarnate with others in and out of our soul group with the agreement that we will help them; and they will help us achieve what we are coming, in human form, to experience, learn, and accomplish. Here is the hard part – when we come into human form, we also come with amnesia. We come into our new human form full of confidence and ready to take on the world. It does not take long for us to forget why we are here. Many of us end up with that bewildered look on our face that asks, who am I? Why am I here? What do I want? Many of us, once exposed to the roadblocks we set up for ourselves, completely lose sight of who we are and why we are here. I always say that it takes a lifetime to remember who we are in spirit and is one of the reasons life on planet Earth is considered so difficult. When we get here, we cannot remember! It is like walking a tightrope blindfolded, composing a musical with no hearing, or creating a piece of pottery without your hands.

Yes, you can do it – you can walk a tightrope using your sense of touch. You can compose a piece of music using the feel of vibration. You can also create a piece of pottery using your feet. You can do it, but it becomes much more difficult. That is life – we can do it, but it is much more difficult than living in spirit where we have and can use additional senses we cannot even imagine on Earth.

I remember once when I was talking to a friend of mine and asking each other some esoteric questions. She asked me, if it were possible, would I like to be able to read other people's minds? I emphatically answered, "NO!" The thought of finding out what people really thought about me or what was really on their minds was too overwhelming to contemplate. Well, as my guides usually do, that night while I was sleeping, they took me to the other side. They showed me what it was like to read their minds. They opened completely and gave me access to what I claimed I did not want. I could read their minds, see, and feel what they thought about me. All I saw and felt was an unconditional love like I had never experienced here on Earth. It was one of the most joyous experiences I have ever had. It showed me the true difference between what we claim is unconditional love here on Earth and what unconditional love truly is. I realized that reading someone's mind while in spirit form was one of the most natural things to experience. In spirit, we have nothing to hide. We are willing to put all our cards on the table, so to speak. In human form, we have so much programming from others throughout our lives that it creates confusion, drama, and a loss of knowing ourselves.

Think about it – from the minute we are born, our parents are teaching us how to behave and about the punishment and reward system. When we are a bit older, we get programming from our siblings, friends, teachers, bosses, and co-workers. They are trying to force their own programming on us! Most of the time it is done and meant with good intentions, but others are trying to show and tell you what works for them, assuming it will work for you too! Sometimes it does and sometimes it does not.

It begins with our parents. They tell us that if we are good, we might get a cookie. If we behave, we might get a hug. If we do not do what they want or expect of us, we will be punished. They might put us in time out. They might take away our toys. They might even spank us. We all learn quickly what is expected of us. Now add teachers, friends, classmates, co-workers, and bosses into the mix. They come from their own programming. Many times, that programming is coming from parents who did not know how to parent because of their own hurtful upbringing. That is all they know, and now they have inflicted that teaching on their own children who are now trying to inflict it upon you! The cycle just goes round and round. Although most parents question their parenting skills from time to time, they still, in many circumstances, will fall back on what they were taught or, in other words, their own programming.

We then get to a point in our lives where we do not know who we are or what we want simply because we have not been allowed to think or act for ourselves. That is when we start to realize we want more. We want something different for ourselves. We now have accumulated enough life experiences to realize there can be a different way. We acknowledge that we are at point A and want to get to point B, but we do not know how to get there. Many times, we are also afraid to decide for fear of being wrong, usually beginning with when we are criticized by our parents or made fun of by our peers. It creates an adult who does not believe themselves worthy enough to make a correct decision.

That is where I come in. A good psychic coach, life coach, or intuitive coach will guide you into making your own decisions. They will give you the tools to help you remember and claim who you really are and help you discover what it is that you really want. You still must do the work, but your coaches will give you the tools to expedite the experience.

Being mindful is a very trendy term right now, but most people do not really know what it means. They think it means being thoughtful. That is certainly part of it, but there is a lot more. To me, being mindful is reversing or reprogramming yourself from things that were told to you or taught to you when you were too young to know that there might be another way. The real definition is WHY DO I DO WHAT I DO AND WHY DO I SAY WHAT I SAY WITHOUT JUDGMENT OF MYSELF OR ANY-BODY ELSE. When we begin to figure that out, we can now, as an adult, decide whether that programming continues to serve us. If not, we release it and let it go. If it does continue to serve us, we hang on to it, but now it becomes a conscious choice.

One of my favorite stories that really explains this point is about a newly married couple. They were hosting a family dinner for the first time and decided to make a ham. The woman pulled the ham out of the refrigerator, cut off both ends of the ham, put it in the pan and then in the oven to bake. Her husband asked her why she cut the ends off the ham. She shrugged her shoulders and said that was the way her mother always did it. When her mother showed up for dinner, the daughter asked her why she always cut the ends off the ham before she cooked it. Her mother just shrugged her shoulders and said it was because that is the way her mother had always done it. Finally, grandma showed up for the family dinner. Her granddaughter, the new wife, asked her, "Grandma? Why did you always cut the ends of the ham off before you cooked it?" The grandmother just looked at her granddaughter and simply said, "So it would fit in my pan."

Who was right and who was wrong? Nobody! Grandma did what she needed to do to get the ham to fit in her pan. Her daughter and granddaughter simply copied that behavior, assuming that was the way you cooked a ham. Now having the real reason why the ends were cut off the ham, the granddaughter realized that way no longer served her, and she could let it go and create her own way. There was no judgment. No one was made to feel right or wrong – a conscious choice was made to change because the young wife realized the real reason of why she did what she did.

So how do you get from point A to point B in the beginning of your journey with mindfulness? When people start this journey, it can be very overwhelming. If you start to question your every thought and every sentence, you will make yourself nuts in no time. That is when most people just give up and walk away. In my opinion, and what seems to work well for myself as well as others I teach, is to just take one thing at a time – after all, you have the rest of your life to work on this! There is no hurry. Begin with things that just seem to fly out of your mouth without really thinking about them. An example might be when you are struggling with your kids. They might ask why, and your quick response might be, "Because I said so!" Is that really the best way to handle that situation? Maybe, but I doubt it. That voice or instant response was most likely coming from a voice you heard many times growing up. After hearing it so many times, it now has become automatic to you too! What you want to do is take a minute and think...and question. Ask yourself if that response to your child is the correct response? If it is, great! You no longer need to question yourself when that comes flying out of your mouth because you have made the conscious decision that it continues to serve both you and your child.

If you find that "Because I said so" might not be the best response, take the time to think of why. Why isn't it the best response? Perhaps because your child no longer responds to a message that really has no meaning behind it? Perhaps because your child does not really understand what that phrase means? Perhaps you are saying it because it has become so automatic from you hearing it so many times in your childhood? Now is the time to think of how you responded when you were a child and heard that same phrase over and over. What impact did it have on you? What impact is it possibly having on your child? Is there a better way to respond? Maybe a better way to respond would be to take the time to answer your child's question of "Why?" I understand that, sometimes in the heat of the moment and after too many "whys", you might be frustrated and want to move on and go about your day. Just know that your child is curious, same as you were at that age. You wanted answers, and so do they! Tell them you will explain later when you have more time. Then you MUST take the time later and go back and explain and answer their question. A child hears, "Because I said so" and can interpret that to mean "shut up" or "you are not worthy of an answer."

Can you see how this can be overwhelming? This is just one instance in a day filled with thousands of thoughts, words, and actions. If you deal with one thing a day, you are already ahead of most people! You are becoming clearer on why you say what you say and do what you do – one thing at a time. Remember, no judgment! Just find a new, better way and let the old way go. The old way did serve you for an awfully long time, but it no longer does; and you now can release it and start your own new programming, which serves you in a new authentic way.

Here is a story that always makes me laugh. An old friend of mine used to keep her light bulbs in the dishtowel drawer. When she purchased them, she would take them out of the corrugated protective packaging and put them between dishtowels in the dishtowel drawer. One day I was helping her clean up after a party, and I reached for a dishtowel and almost pulled out a light bulb at the same time, which would have sent it flying across the room to its certain demise. I looked at her with an incredulous look on my face and asked what the heck the light bulbs were doing in the dishtowel drawer! She told me her mother had always put them there to protect the light bulbs. They were safe in that drawer. Huh? I almost accidentally hurled one across the room! What was she talking about? Come to find out this was another habit that had been passed down through generations before light bulbs were sold in protective wrapping. Each generation continued this habit even after light bulbs came wrapped in corrugated cardboard. I started laughing as I pointed out the obvious to my friend, and she just shrugged her shoulders and went about her business. To this day, I do not know if she continues that habit or if she released it and has found a new way to store her light bulbs. See? There was no judgment. Laughter, yes, but no judgment once we both recognized the reason she did what she did. Did it continue to serve her? Only she could answer that question and make that decision.

I always tell people that the journey to self-awareness will be the most joyous journey you will ever take, but that does not mean it will be easy. Life is life. It is filled with roadblocks, pain, sorrow, and loss, in addition to joy, happiness, and peace. It is not what happens to you; it is how you react to what happens to you. Self-awareness is the best way to make conscious choices and decisions to make your life the best life it can be. We all deserve joyful and happy lives. It is time to claim yours! Self-awareness will help you have the resilience you need and want to live your best life and be the next best version of you.

Why Earth Instead of Other Planets

Why do we come to Earth in the first place? Life is not easy on this planet, so why do we come here, let alone choose to come here? Some days, months, or years feel like punishment from a God with a sadistic side.

It is my understanding that Earth truly is one of the harshest planets. Earth is a school, an extremely hard school. Because we come to Earth with little or no memory of who we are in spirit, it is easy to lose our way. That is the point! Earth is nothing but a school. It is also a hard, dense planet – in fact, it is my understanding, the hardest and densest of all the planets.

If we are all one and we are all a piece of God, the Creator, or Source, we really cannot lose our way. Our main purpose is to do our part of experiencing everything that has ever been or ever will be. Planet Earth appears to be just one of the places available to accomplish that. It also offers our souls a huge opportunity for growth that no other planet can.

I recommend, if you have not, that you read Dolores Cannon's books. She spent decades as a hypnotherapist and teacher dedicated to understanding our origins as human beings as well as our existence before and after Earth. She claims that being human is a process and that we must go through all levels of energy of life before we can express ourselves as a human being. We might begin our energy existence on planet Earth by being a rock. Yes, a rock! If Earth is a living, breathing expression of energy, so is everything on or in it, including rocks. So, we might begin life as a rock, and when we have learned everything that a rock needs to learn, we simply leave that existence. The next incarnation might be as plant life. After that, perhaps as a fairy or gnome. Then an animal. Hopefully, this will answer the question of whether some of these things merely exist or whether they have souls or consciousness. Of course, they do. They cannot exist without a soul or consciousness! After we have gone through the stages listed here, we are ready to be human. There are exceptions, of course, but most people will live many lives so they can experience what it is like to be every gender and every ethnicity. They will also repeat over and over again certain genders and certain ethnicities until they learn what they wanted to learn in that particular lifetime. Fascinating, isn't it? In those different incarnations we experience prejudice, racism, judgment, and other things that make our planet unique. This has been my belief system for decades and gives me the perspective to watch people's judgment of others when it is different from themselves. It really makes no sense! If you have been a human from another race or country, how can you be prejudice? If you have not yet experienced life as a particular race, get ready – you will! How will it feel to be judged for a skin color or an accent or some other perceived difference? All I am saying is that this is part of the Karmic wheel. How you judge or hurt others will come back to you in another life with a similar experience. We are all human in this life. We are here for the same reason: to learn and experience. The choice is yours – do you want to learn love, kindness, and respect or do you want to learn pain, hate, and fear?

By choosing Earth we give ourselves the challenges to achieve goals, learn lessons, and experience life. We can feel separate. We can feel alone. How do we survive with this feeling of separateness? It is a lifetime pursuit to remember who we are in spirit, that we are never alone, and that we have a huge team on the other side rooting for us! The other side understands what a challenge it is for everyone to live a life here on Earth, let alone learn the lessons we came here to learn.

One of the first times I underwent hypnosis, my hypnotherapist told me to go back to where my issue started. What she intended was for me to go back to the beginning of the issue I came to see her about, which was alien contact. Well, something else entirely happened. I went back to a bright pink planet! I remember seeing this planet, which felt like it was covered in water. Pink water. I felt like a little fairy person whose wings fluttered as I flew around what appeared to be my home. The sheer joy of dipping my toe in the water and watching the water ripple brought me more joy than I have ever experienced on Earth. The hypnotherapist asked me where I was. The only answer I could provide was home. I am home. She asked me if this planet had a name. I told her its name was home. It was my first home as a conscious life form. She then asked what I saw around me. As I looked around, I saw several different planets so vibrant in color yet easy on my eyesight. They looked close enough to reach out and touch. Then planet Earth came into focus from a distance. It had this aura of polluted brown around it, and I immediately began to cry. I felt the pain, hurt, anger, and mistreatment of the planet. The energy was so painful to "see."

The questions arose of why we treat each other so poorly. Why does hate even exist on this planet? What was the purpose? What is there to gain by acting the way people do on planet Earth? It broke my heart to experience that kind of energy, especially when a few seconds earlier I felt nothing but joy when simply dipping my toe in water. The simple things bring the most joy. I believe that to be true on my home pink planet as well as planet Earth.

The messages received as to why earthlings behave as they do became clear. The people on Earth are there for a very specific reason. The reason is just another avenue to experience a piece of whatever has happened and whatever will happen. The Earth experience of expressing happens to be contained on planet Earth because that kind of pain, hurt, and anger would not be allowed to exist anywhere else. As we become closer and closer to destroying our planet, a new breed of children is being born to help educate the earlier souls and do what they can to reverse the damage already done to this beautiful planet.

We need to listen to the younger generations for they come with a new agenda, a purpose to undo what we have done. Many are old souls that are here on a mission: to save us and save our home. We are the only species willing to destroy their own home.

That is why we have come to planet Earth. With the multitude of other lives we have lived, many have been on planet Earth, but others have been on planets in and out of our solar system. When we choose other planets, it is to learn other lessons more conducive to that planet. Believe me, there are planets, like my pink planet, that are nothing but peace, calm, and love. There are other planets that are even more violent than Earth and others in between.

If any of you decide to have a past life regression done, most regressionists will focus on your lives on planet Earth. This is great because learning about past lives is always enlightening. Occasionally, you will get a regressionist who will hit upon lives on other planets. If you are open to such an experience – go for it! It will blow your mind in ways you cannot even imagine.

In another regression session I experienced after the pink planet session, my hypnotherapist told me to go back to the beginning, believing I would head right back to the pink planet. Not so fast! All I saw was darkness. I waited for something else to show up, but nothing did. I was beginning to get nervous and told the hyp-notherapist what I was seeing, or rather what I was not seeing. She told me to move forward in time until I did see something. Suddenly, the darkness was filled with a billion stars. Yes, it felt like I was experiencing the big bang! I felt my soul shining like a star in the night sky. As I looked around, I saw a few other souls that I recognized from my current Earth life. It became clear that the pink planet was my first home as a spirit but not where I was born. You can equate it to being born in a hospital, but your first home is where your parents took you when leaving the hospital.

So, choosing a human experience on planet Earth for this lifetime is powerful, but that lifetime is just a spark in the energy that is you. You have been around forev-er and lived on various other planets in addition to your many incarnations on Earth! It might be a small world, but it is a huge universe!

Because we choose the lessons we want to learn when we come to Earth, it is like writing a script for a play. We choose it, we write it, we live it. The main point is that we can re-write the script anytime we choose; anytime life is not going the way we want, we can re-write it. You witness this all the time, don't you? Think about addicts. They can be in the throes of addiction and de-cide to live life a different way. They can get help for this re-write by entering rehab, leaning on friends, or quitting cold turkey. In other words – they have re-writ-ten their script!

Earth is also the only planet that has free will and is a living, evolving being – just like we are as human beings! Because we have free will, I have come to un-derstand that when Earth was originally populated, it was with the agreement that there would be no inter-ference. Human beings were given free will to create, live, evolve, or destroy their home. It is entirely up to us. The only way beings from other planets can interfere is if we are on the brink of destruction, the brink of destroying ourselves, because the destruction of Earth would be devastating to the entire solar system. There is a balance that cannot be disrupted, and therefore, earthlings can do as they please up to a point – the point of destroying themselves.

When certain inventions were discovered, several people often came forward within days of each other with the same or similar invention. That is because Earth is given certain ideas or information to help evolution. The ideas are floating out there, and it is up to individuals to claim those ideas and bring them to fruition, which is why so many things can happen simultaneously. Multiple people grab the idea and make it happen! The information is out there for anybody, but it is usually the people skilled in a particular area, such as tangible items, medical cures, poetry, and music, that make it happen.

Here is the thing – when ideas are put into our consciousness, it is with the curiosity of how humans will bring it into public consciousness, or rather how they will use this information. The one item that drove this home to me was 3-D printing. This idea was brought into consciousness, and I immediately thought of creating prosthetic limbs. Amazing! So, what was the first thing I saw being created with 3-D printing? A gun. Really? That is how free will works. We are given the information or idea and then it is up to us to use that information in whatever way we choose. Do we use it to help others on our planet to live a better or easier life? Or do we use it to destroy? The choice is ours – it is always ours.

Auras and chakras

What is an aura? What are chakras? Most people have heard of an aura, but not as many are familiar with chakras. Let us begin with chakras. Chakras are the energy centers in the body. There are seven main chakras: root, sacral, solar plexus, heart, throat, third eye, and crown.

Science has proven that everything is energy – that includes our chakras. The energy from our chakras radiates out of our body, creating our aura. It is as simple as that! Well, not really. Let us go back to each chakra, shall we?

The Root Chakra – The root chakra is located at the base of the spine. The color associated with the root chakra is red. This energy center in your body is to keep you centered and grounded in life.

The Sacral Chakra – The sacral chakra is located below your navel. The color associated with your sacrum is orange. This energy center in your body is the foundation of passion, sexual organs, and creativity.

The Solar Plexus Chakra – The solar plexus is located just above your navel. The color associated with your solar plexus is yellow. This energy center in your body is your sense of self.

The Heart Chakra – The heart chakra is in the middle of your chest. The color associated with the heart chakra is green. This energy center is for love, compassion, and caring.

The Throat Chakra – The throat chakra is in the throat area just above your thyroid. The color associated with the throat is light blue. This energy center in your body is your ability to speak your truth.

The Third Eye Chakra – The third eye chakra is located between and just above your eyebrows. The color associated with your third eye is indigo. It represents intuition or your ability to tune into certain persons, places, or things.

The Crown Chakra – The crown chakra is located at the top of the head. The color associated with the crown is purple. This energy center in your body is your connection to spirit.

When our chakras vibrate with energy as they always do, it radiates through and out of our body, creating an aura. Many people can see auras; many people cannot. It really does not make any difference – just know that your aura is there. Your aura will also radiate different colors, which stem from the chakras. Almost everyone's aura will represent all colors of the chakras, but many will have a dominate color or two, representing the chakras strongest at that moment in time. If you ever get the chance to experience aura photography, do it! It is fascinating as well as educational. Most aura photographers will offer a breakdown of your dominant colors and what they mean for you. Some photographers will also show pictures of your chakras, which is even more fascinating. For instance, if your aura photo shows a dominate yellow color, it would be associated with your solar plexus or your sense of self and would indicate you have a strong sense of who you are in the human experience at that time. Your aura colors are constantly changing depending on what you are going through at that moment. A joke I like to make on days that I am feeling a bit down or just out of sorts is that my aura is a filthy brown today! So, no, I know my aura is not a filthy brown just like I know yours is not either – it is just a way to have some fun. Spirituality is supposed to be fun as we chose to come here as a human and deal with all of this. We might as well have some fun with all the craziness!

So, let us say your aura photo shows a weak blue color or no blue at all. Blue, as we discussed earlier, is associated with your throat or speaking your truth. If blue is weak for you, that means you might want to focus on speaking your truth. Many times, when I am doing a Reiki session, I will spot issues with the throat chakra. It usually means that the client, even if they feel like they speak their truth now, have not always felt that way. It can go back to childhood when "children should be seen and not heard" was still the standard. I always say that the body tells the truth. You can run, but you cannot hide from your body! Aura photography is a wonderful way to get to the truth of what your body is trying to tell you.

As I was developing my psychic and medium gifts, I used to get my aura photo taken every year at about the same time so I could monitor any changes. Wow, were there changes! The colors were becoming brighter and more distinct. The chakras began taking on specific shapes. By shapes, I mean they began looking like little spaceships! Those of you who read my second book, *We Are Not Alone…My Extraterrestrial Contact,* will know that I have had abduction experiences most of my life. As I began to really develop and work with my psychic gifts, my chakras were telling a story, too. I have always wondered whether I am psychic because of my abduction experiences or if I was chosen to be abducted because I am psychic. I have decided that I became psychic because of my abduction experiences, but I may never know the truth until I, too, am on the other side.

Our energy centers begin with our chakras, but that is only the beginning! There are many, many other chakras in our bodies but are in a less dominate form.

There are also what we call meridians. Our meridians are basically our energetic highway. The main chakras send out energy to the smaller chakras, which then send that energy out to the meridians, or our energetic highway, to keep our bodies running smoothly. When the chakras get clogged, slow down, or start spinning in the wrong direction, that's when alternative energy work comes in. I like to equate alternative energy work, in particular Reiki, to going to the dentist. We all brush our teeth every day, but there is still a build-up of plaque that calls for a trip to the dentist to get our teeth cleaned. This is similar to what Reiki is to the body. We can eat right, exercise, and take care of ourselves, but everyday living can affect our chakras. Noise pollution, air pollution, florescent lighting, etc. can all slow down the functions of our chakras without our even knowing it. When you start to feel out of sorts, slow, not motivated, or even just stuck, that is usually a particularly good time to seek out an alternative healing method to assist those chakras in performing as they are meant to so the body can heal itself.

Many times, I am asked why Reiki or any alternative energy work is needed if the body can heal itself. That is an easy question to answer. If you cut yourself, the body heals itself, doesn't it? You might need surgery to remove a foreign object, but ultimately the body still heals itself. Part of the healing process is to remove obstacles, whether they be physical or emotional, so the body can heal itself. The trick is to find the right doctor or alternative practitioner to assist you and your body so it can function in the way it is supposed to and heal itself.

Keep those chakras clean and clear, people! Let your body function in its most efficient way!

The Clairs

We are all familiar with our five physical senses, correct? Taste, touch, smell, sight, and sound. Well, we all have psychic senses, too! As you tune into your spirit guides and your spiritual life, you will become more aware and comfortable with your psychic senses, which are known as The Clairs. They are clairvoyance (clear seeing), clairaudience (clear hearing), claircognizance (clear knowing), clairsentience (clear feeling), clairgustance (clear tasting), clairalience (clear smelling).

Let us look at them in greater detail:

Clairvoyance/clear seeing – This happens to be my strongest psychic sense in that I see pictures. When spirit sends pictures to me, I see with my third eye or inside my head; I do not see with my physical eyes. When I work with clients, I usually ask them what was the easiest for them to learn when they were in school. Did they learn when they saw something on the chalkboard? Did they need to listen to the teacher explain things? Did they have an innate understanding of the subject? Or did they need to touch something, take it apart, and put it back together to really understand? When the client answers that they learned best when seeing something on a chalkboard, the clair strongest for them will most likely be clairvoyance. We then begin to develop their psychic senses by focusing on their third eye or what is going on inside their head.

When I do readings for people, I always tell them that the information I get is correct, but I might not be able to translate the picture I am getting correctly and, therefore, might need their validation or clarification. For instance, in one reading, the client's father came through for me. He showed me a can of cherry pie filling. I was not sure how to interpret that picture, so I simply asked my client why his dad would be showing me a can of cherry pie filling. My client said his dad would show me that picture for two reasons: 1) cherry pie was his favorite pie and 2) when my client was younger, his dad was helping him with his spelling homework and happened to spell cherry wrong. That is why my client's dad did not just show me a pie or a spelling chart – there was more to it than that! Instead, he chose to send me a picture of the can of cherry pie filling, knowing I would ask my client to clarify for me. This is what I call a multi-level message. When you tune in to your third eye, simply ask your guides to send pictures to assist you in developing the clair of clairvoyance. Clairvoyance is a bit like playing Charades since you must interpret the picture or symbol that is being sent to you.

Clairaudience/clear hearing – The amazing thing about this clair is that you can hear internal noises as well as external noises. Internal noises might sound like a random song popping in your head. Just like clairvoyance, the sound is inside your head. I am sure many of you, just as you are going to sleep at night, have heard someone shout your name. That is usually a guide or a deceased loved one stopping by to say hello.

During one reading with a mother who had lost her only child, I kept hearing "sister, sister." I asked my client if she had lost another child. She emphatically told me no. I asked her why I kept hearing the word sister and her deceased son saying he was watching over his little sister. My client looked a bit shocked but did tell me that her ex-husband had remarried, and they had a little girl who was her son's half-sister. That message, even though I heard it, was still inside my head. In other words, you will hear with your head, not your ears.

The way you might experience external sound is overhearing a conversation between people whether in person, on the radio, or television. When the dialog catches your attention – pay attention! There is a message there for you. You might also hear sounds coming from a clock, for instance. The ticking of the clock might represent the passing of time, an appointment for which you are late, or a sense of urgency. It is what I like to call a forced connection. Spirits are forcing you to notice something as a sign or message to you.

Claircognizance/clear knowing – Have you ever had the experience of just knowing something but not really knowing how you knew it – you just knew it? That's claircognizance at work for you. I like to equate claircognizance with mother's intuition. When a child is hurt many times, a mother just knows there is something wrong and will jump into action.

Clairsentience/clear feeling – This is how YOUR intuition communicates with you. Have you ever walked into a party and felt the energy was off somehow? Have you ever met someone and instinctively knew you liked them and could trust them? How about the opposite? You met someone and your gut just told you to give them a wide berth? That is clairsentience warning you of trouble ahead or letting you know everything is good and you can progress with this person, thing, or event.

Clairgustance/clear tasting – Shortly after my mother passed away, I was walking through the grocery store and passed an item of food that was her favorite. I could automatically taste the special way she prepared that food and the unique taste it left in my mouth. It was at that time I knew my mother was close by me and sending me messages. Although this is one of the less common clairs, it can be a strong message that someone you loved who has passed over is near you and sending you messages of love and peace. Sometimes, during a reading with someone, I will taste blood in my mouth. That is usually my symbol that the person died tragically and there was blood loss involved.

Clairalience/clear smelling – Again, this is not a common clair but still can be sending you very distinct messages. For instance, my father was a heavy smoker most of his life. After he passed, I would smell the strong odor of cigarettes around me, and I knew it was him. Now, as much as I loved my father, I could not stand the smell of cigarettes. I still did not like it even though it was coming from the other side! I asked my father to please use a different way of communicating with me rather than that horrid smoke! Perfume is a quite common way to communicate using clairalience. Remember grandma's favorite perfume? Next time you smell it, you can trust that it is her saying hello.

You might notice that one clair is stronger than another, which is usually the case, especially when you are first learning to develop your clairs. What I found is after becoming very comfortable with my clairvoyance, the other clairs started to kick in. Now, with practice, they are all strong, and it is up to me to pay attention! It also depends on the spirit sending the messages. They might be more comfortable sending pictures rather than sound. They might realize that you will respond in a stronger way if they send the scent of the cologne they always wore. Getting messages from spirit is always a two-way street. Not only is it how we receive messages, but it is also how they choose to send them to us, which can vary spirit to spirit.

Spirit Guides

What are spirit guides and why do we need them? To me, spirit guides represent the highest form of truth and compassion that help keep us in alignment with the universe. Pretty simple, but profound. In the metaphysical area, there are varying opinions on everything including spirit guides, so what I am giving you here comes from my own experience and my own years of study.

The most frequent question I get concerning spirit guides is what is the difference between Angels and spirit guides? Good question! In my opinion, Angels are from the angelic realm and also there to guide us, but they are energy that has never been in human form.

Spirit guides have lived many lives and bring that expertise to guide us in our current human life. We usually know our guides on a spirit or soul level, so we are familiar with each other. We have perhaps even switched places and been a guide to them in one of their human experiences!

Another question I get is, "Can my deceased loved one be my guide?" Usually, the answer is no, unless that deceased loved one died before you were born or when you were young. There are always exceptions, but typically what I have found is that spirit guides are only known to us in the spirit realm. We generally do not know or remember them when they were in a human body.

So, why do we need spirit guides? When we are in spirit, we make a life plan. That plan consists of lessons we want to learn, things we want to experience, and goals we want to accomplish. Many of us choose a life plan that can be difficult, so we need reinforcements to help us do what we came here to do. An example of this might be if you lived in New York and wanted to drive to California. Would you use a map? Would you use a GPS system of some kind or would you just jump in your car and start driving and hope for the best? Any way you choose is right, but would it be easier to have a guidance system of some kind in place? That guidance system will show you where detours are, where highways vs interstates are, etc. Your car's guidance system makes it easier to get where you are going!

Can that guidance system tell you to go to Montana instead of California because you might have more fun there? No, it cannot! It will show you the easiest way to get to California where you said you wanted to go. Now, if you change your mind and say, "Well, maybe I want to go to Montana on my way to California." You simply reprogram your GPS to take you to Montana first and then on to California, and your GPS will do exactly that. That is where free will comes into play. You can make it a straight shot to get to California, or when we talk about your life plan, you can make it a straight shot to learn and accomplish what you came here to learn. Otherwise, you can take what I like to call the scenic route and experience other things along the way to your destination. How cool is that?! It is always your choice.

Another thing I hear frequently from clients is that they do not want to bug their guides, perhaps their guides are busy. Really? No way! It is like telling your GPS to take some time off while you just drive on your own. Yes, you can certainly do that, but your GPS is there to do a job and so are your guides. Their job is one and the same – to get you where you say you want to go.

How many spirit guides do you have? My experience tells me that most people typically have between three and seven guides at any one time. We all have a main guide with us from the time we are born until the time we die. The other guides step forward and backward as we go through changes in our lives. A great example of this is the first time someone finds out they are going to be a parent. Typically, there will be a guide who steps forward to guide you into taking care of your baby in the best way possible. Can you ignore your guides? Absolutely! But why would you want to when they are the highest form of truth and compassion? Listen to them! Pay attention to them!

When I do readings for people, I will usually see three guides. If a client is going through something particularly trying or stressful like the loss of a child or spouse, I will see up to seven guides around them. Just know you are never alone. Even at your lowest times, you are never alone. Your guides are there to comfort you and guide you back into alignment with the universe.

How do you connect with your guides?

There are so many ways to connect with your guides. You can try all kinds of different ways, see which way works best for you, and use that way exclusively or you can try different ways at different times. Personally, I use a mixture of ways to connect just to keep it interesting!

To me, the easiest way to connect to your guides is to close your eyes and sit in a comfortable position in a quiet place where you will not be interrupted, at least for the first time. After that you will find connecting with them to be a natural part of your day's activities.

Now that your eyes are closed, out loud, ask the following: I want to connect with my main spirit guide. Are you male or female? You should have an answer before you finish asking the question. That is where most people get frustrated or confused. They are used to communicating the way we do in human form on Earth – we ask a question and then wait for an answer. Nope, that is not the way I find that it works in the spirit world. You will have an answer usually before the first three words are out of your mouth. If there is a tricky part, here it is – I do not know how you will receive the information. You might see a picture, you might hear something, or you might just have a gut sensation of knowing. However, you do not see those pictures with your eyes; you see them with your head. You do not hear with your ears; you hear with your head. That gut feeling may just feel like something odd is happening in your stomach or you get a sensation of knowing. Do not second guess yourself! Trust the information you are getting!!! Second guessing would be like when your GPS tells you to turn left and you think, nah, it does not know what it is doing. I am turning right because I know better. Trust, trust, trust! I also tell people that, in the beginning, listening to your guides is like listening to a feather fall through air. You really do have to pay attention until their voices or energy are as familiar to you as your best friend's. Then you will understand them clearly just like you would recognize your best friend's voice anywhere.

Sometimes when you ask if they are male or female, you might not get a response, or you will get both male and female. Remember, your guides have lived many, many lifetimes and have been every gender and every ethnicity. They might decide not to show you a gender. Again, trust the information you are getting! I begin with that question so you can get used to how that guide will communicate with you and how you will receive their messages.

The next question you want to ask them is, "What can I call you?" So many people expect a very exotic name, and sometimes that is what you will receive. Most of the time, however, your guides will give you a name that is simple and easy to remember. People are always surprised when a simple name comes to them and comes easily. They think they are making it up. Trust me you are not! Even if you are making it up, who cares?! Your guides certainly do not. Remember, they have had so many lives and so many different lives and different names to go with those lives that they really do not care what you call them. You can even begin your contact with your guides by calling them your team, which ensures you are including all guides that are with you at that given time.

I remember when I first decided to contact my main guide. I understood that it was a male and saw that he had somewhat of an alien Desmond Tutu look about him. I asked what I could call him and here is approximately what he gave me Mexxiu#$%*&#@)(%^*. I said, "Really? You have got to be kidding! I cannot even pronounce that! Is there a shorter version of that or a nickname I can call you instead?" He told me to just use the first two letters. Ok, I can do that. M – e. Me. Me? I just started laughing. Really, how true is it that our main guide should be a version of ourselves? It certainly is true for me!

After you have contacted your main guide, you will want to move on and connect to at least two others. Begin with saying that you want to connect with the guide over your left shoulder. Ask if they are male or female. When you get your answer, make sure to thank them. After you get a gender (or not), then ask what you can call them. Your next question to them is what is their main purpose in being your guide in this lifetime. You will find that it gets easier and easier to understand what they are communicating to you as you realize how they are connecting to you. Is it visually? Is it auditory? Is it a sense of just knowing? When you understand the dominate way your spirit guides are communicating with you, it will be much easier to tap into them.

When you have received the information from the guide over your left shoulder, do the same with the guide over your right shoulder. What is your gender? What can I call you? What is your main purpose in being my guide in this lifetime? Always thank your guides for the information they give to you.

I begin each morning with a short meditation. I thank my guides, by name, for the day that lies ahead. I also thank them for clear messages I need to hear that day for my healing and highest good. To be clear, there are many days I accuse my guides of drinking on the job. Sometimes their messages do not make any sense to me or seem just plain wrong! I learned a long time ago, however, that spirit never lets you down. I now trust the information my guides are giving me even if it makes no sense at the time. The messages always make sense down the road.

Just think back on your life. Job changes, relationship changes, life decisions. How many of them were truly wrong? I am betting none of them were wrong because they you where you are today. Even if you have had a checkered past, you learned, you grew, and you blossomed into the person you wanted to be. Or you are still on that path and are continuing to blossom into the person you want to be.

Getting to be authentically you is a lifelong journey. Do not forget that. We all are constantly changing even if we do not realize it at the time. We are not done or complete with change until we decide to leave this human body. Even then, our soul still changes and evolves, just not our human body. We are energy, and energy does not die; it merely changes form.

When you have a good relationship with your spirit

guides, you will never be alone again. You never were alone, but at least now you know it. Your spirit guides become your best friends. Greet them every morning and thank them every night. Your relationship with anyone, whether it be spirit guides, friends, or family, should be an even energy exchange. It is all give and take. Your guides want to help you. They want nothing more than to see you achieve what you came to planet Earth to achieve. Let them help you!

I do need to clarify that your guides are there to help you achieve what you came her to achieve. They can help, but they cannot interfere. A way to explain this is let us say that part of your life plan is to be in a bad car accident. Your guides cannot prevent that from happening, but they can arrange for the car behind you to have a doctor in it or that the accident happens near a hospital. They can help, but they cannot interfere! I cannot stress that loudly enough.

One wonderful thing I discovered about my spirit guides is that they have a well-developed sense of humor. In my case, my guides are just plain twisted with their humor! It sometimes feels like they are running a very sophomoric fraternity house instead of guiding me through my life's purpose. Do not dismiss messages from your guides simply because the information they deliver is funny. Those are the best messages! Life is meant to be fun! Yes, we are here to learn lessons, and many of them are hard and very painful. That does not mean all of life has to be that way. In between painful lessons, have fun! Enjoy life! You deserve a happy and joyful life. Did you know that? You are the creator of your own life. You are the designer of your own life, and you can make it look however you choose. Are you living a life that makes you feel fulfilled? Are you happy? Are you the person you want to be? You have control over all these things! Do you believe you deserve a happy and joyful life? I am here to tell you that you do! You deserve every wild dream you have had about yourself. Now it is up to you to claim it. Your guides are here to help you do just that. All you must do is ask and then believe it is possible.

Life Plan and Soul Groups

So, what is a life plan? When we are in spirit form and preparing to come to Earth in human form, we create a plan for ourselves. At a very high level, what we are designing are the lessons we want to learn, things we want to experience, and goals we want to accomplish.

We cannot do this alone, so we also work with other spirits that are part of our soul group and our extended soul group. Together we agree to help each other along the way to learn those lessons. What is a soul group? A soul group is a group of souls who will reincarnate together over and over, always changing roles. All of this is to assist each other in the evolution of our souls with the ultimate goal of enlightenment. The definition of enlightenment is that everything you think, say, or do comes from love – not from fear.

I do not know about you, but just when I think I am making good progress in this lifetime, I check in with my higher self to see if everything I think, say, or do is truly coming from love. Although I really am making progress, it is usually a sobering experience to recognize how much of what I think, say, and do still comes from fear. I do have to say that I am getting better at recognizing it and shifting the programming of fear into love, or at the very least, into neutrality.

Because we do not know what anyone else's life plan is when they come to Earth, we have no right to judge it. We must trust that they are doing it perfectly even if it does not match our own life plan. We must trust that we are doing it perfectly too. While on Earth, we cannot judge ourselves either. All we can do is ask ourselves, "Am I happy?" If you can answer that question with a resounding YES, you are doing what you came here to do. If there is any questioning or if you have the empty feeling in the pit of your stomach, there is still work to be done. It does not mean you are not on the right path, but it can mean that it is time to make some changes. Our lives zig and zag as long as we live. It does not mean we are doing things wrong; it just means we are ready for the next step or the next adventure.

Here is an interesting thing to consider – the person who is or has been a major pain in your backside just might be part of your soul group and is acting the part of the villain to help you learn one of the many lessons you came here to learn. That boss that fired you? That friend that betrayed you? That lover or spouse who cheated? They very well could be part of your soul group and are playing the part of the protagonist or the bad guy to help you learn what you **do not** want in a relationship or job. They could very well be your greatest teacher helping you get a job that better suits you or find a new mate that is a much better match to you. We can get complacent in life – many people struggle with change. Our so-called enemies are here to help us along. They are here to push us into the next zig or zag and get us moving along our path again.

You really cannot get your life path wrong, but you can go through life and not learn what you came here to learn or accomplish. That does not mean you failed. It simply means you will have to come back into human form and try again…and again…and again until those lessons are learned. You see, we live on a free will planet, meaning although we came here with specific things to learn and do, we do not necessarily take the steps to make them happen. A great example is childhood trauma. We all have had trauma to one degree or another. At some point in our lives, however, we must decide if we are the victim or the survivor. I see so many people who are content to live their lives as a victim, and the excuse is always the same – my mother, my father, my whomever. The list can go on and on, blaming someone else for their own misfortunes. It appears easier to blame someone or something else for our troubles, but doing it that way during a lifetime is exhausting.

You also hear stories of people overcoming insurmountable odds to achieve great things in life. They took the challenges they had set up for themselves and said, "NO! Just watch me!" They said, "I have dreams, and nothing is going to get in my way of achieving those dreams." There might have been things that slowed them down, but those things did not stop these lovely souls.

I will bet you are wondering about the challenges they set up for themselves, right? It is true. We set the lessons, we set the goals, we set the dreams. We also set the challenges for ourselves. Again, our besties in the spirit world, our soul group, are here to be those challenges. They are also here to be our biggest cheerleaders.

When it is our turn to transition out of our human body and go back to spirit, we are not judged by others. We are only judged by ourselves. Truly, how can we be judged by others when others did not set the lessons, goals, or experiences? We only judge ourselves with what we came to Earth to do and to what degree we did those things. I have discovered through my own experiences that we really do not judge ourselves on how much money we made, how big our house was, or even what kind of car we drove. Those are very material things that can make our lives easier or more comfortable, but they are not the things that create our character. Our character is created by how we treat and love others and ourselves. Yes, we must love ourselves. For how can we love others if we do not know how or if we refuse to love ourselves? We cannot. It is that simple. For all our mistakes and misguided steps, we are learning and evolving. If there is any judging to be done, we should be judged with accolades and pats on the back for a good effort! A good start! We are all one; we are all part of a magnificent universe. After our human lives, we will go back to source from whence we came. We are part of the whole. Is one part of that whole better than another part? Absolutely not. We all come to Earth for the same reason – to evolve. We have chosen different ways to do that, and all ways need to be honored even if we do not understand to-day. When it comes our time to rejoin source, we will have a perfect understanding.

source, soul and spirit

In my world, there is a huge difference between source, soul, and spirit, and yet there is no difference at all. Hmm, how does that work? If you think of the ocean, for instance, a single drop of water from the ocean is still the ocean, but it is identified as a single drop of water. If you put that single drop of water in a bucket of ocean water, it is still a drop of water; but it is now also part of a bucket of water and yet it is still the ocean. If you put that bucket of water in the ocean, that single drop of water still exists; the bucket of water still exists but it is now part of the whole – the ocean!

That is how we tell the difference between source, soul, and spirit. In this human experience, you are a single spirit, but you come from source. To me, Source is God, the Creator, or the Source of everything that has ever been or ever will be.

We separate from source (the ocean) as a soul (the bucket of water), which then separates into individual spirits, one of which is you now in this human incarnation (single drop of water). So, what do I mean when I say your soul separates into individual spirits? This is what I refer to as parallel lives (more on parallel lives in another chapter). Your soul can separate into individual spirits so you can live other lives at the same time (parallel lives)! The thing is, those lives might not all be on Earth as we know it. Your other lives might be happening on different planets, different galaxies, or different universes…all at the same time. Yes, this can be awfully hard to wrap your head around, which is why I am leaving a deeper explanation for another chapter.

So, let us look at things from a different perspective. If we are all one – source – why am I different from you? Why are you different from your parents? How can we all be different from each other if we are all one – source? The answer is simple yet complex. Ego is what separates us.

If source is everything that has ever been and ever will be, why do we exist as individuals at all? In my experience, we exist to experience everything that has ever been and everything that ever will be. That means you come from source to experience one thing and I come from source to experience something else. Our egos are what help us do that or, in other words, experience what we came here to experience.

Ego maniac or ego run amok is a completely different thing. I am talking about the healthy ego with which we were born. A definition of ego is the part of the mind that mediates between the conscious and the unconscious and is responsible for reality testing and a sense of personal identity. Also, in metaphysics, ego is considered a conscious thinking subject. You see? We separate ourselves from source and form a personal identity to experience a portion of everything that has ever been or ever will be. When what we have agreed to experience in this human consciousness in this human life is complete, we transition or die and return to our soul. When all our lives as spirit are complete, we return to our soul, which then returns to source.

Since everything is energy, we do not really die – we simply change form by shedding our human body and letting our spirit return to its natural form of energy and return home or back to source.

So why does source exist? Why does source want to experience everything that has ever been and ever will be? I do not know. Maybe I will have the answer by the time I write my next book! For now, I have only been given the information that source does exist. Why? I do not know.

Another thing I really want to make clear is that if some-one tells you they know the absolute answer to every-thing regarding life...they are wrong. Until we are on the other side, no one knows for sure what source is, what God is, what the creator is, who we are, and why we are here. I am only writing things from my perspec-tive, my experiences and what spirit has come through to tell me from the other side.

As I mentioned earlier, I was engaged to a man many years ago who passed away from melanoma. On the way to his funeral, I asked him to let me know that he was ok. I felt his warm hand on my shoulder as he told me to turn on the radio. As I turned on the radio to my favorite station, the song *From a Distance* by Bette Midler was playing. It was truly the perfect song for me to know it was from him and sent directly to me.

A few weeks after his passing I awoke one morning realizing my alarm had not gone off and I would be late for work. I jumped out of bed and headed directly to the shower. As the spray from the water hit my body, mem-ories came flooding back into my consciousness. Mike came during the night and took me to the other side. He and I were sitting on a riverbank with the sound and feel of crunchy fall leaves around us. We were discussing religion and spirituality. When he was alive, this was something we vehemently disagreed about. He was from a strict Catholic upbringing, and although I was raised with organized religion, it was not part of my current belief system. For once, we were discussing religion and spirituality with a complete understanding of each other's beliefs and practices. He looked alive; he looked healthy and happy like I had not seen him look in a very long time.

I asked him what he did in Heaven and he told me he was taking classes. What? You can imagine my sur-prise to hear that he was taking classes. I was not sure at that time what people did on the other side or in Heaven, where we hope all loved ones go, but I was certainly surprised to hear that they could study!

I asked him what he was studying, and he said that he could not tell me because I did not have the capacity to understand. I begged a bit, and he finally relented with the understanding that my memory would have to be erased after I was told. I readily agreed, never dreaming he could actually erase my memory. Once he told me what he was studying, I remember being shocked because everything sounded very sci-fi and certainly nothing that could happen on planet Earth.

I asked him where he was taking the classes, and he pointed to a smallish building that looked like a house outlined with clear twinkle lights, except there was no house! It was just the outline of a house. I also saw what appeared to be shooting stars entering the building from the top and sides as well as the imagined front door. I asked Mike about the shooting stars, and he told me those were his fellow students. I told him how happy I was that he really was good, healthy, happy, and appearing to be alive. He was much like the Mike I knew and loved, only he was so at peace now. He did not have life getting in the way of his being happy. The next thing I remember is waking up noticing the malfunctioning alarm clock. All the memories came flooding back in the shower that day except what Mike was studying. Yes, he had indeed erased my memory.

As a psychic medium, I now understand when a client's loved one comes through with messages of what they are doing on the other side. Without the experience with Mike that night, I doubt if I would truly understand what they were trying to convey.

At night we all astral travel. Most of us just do not remember. Our bodies need rest, but our souls do not. I surely do not remember even a fraction of what I get to experience during my night travels, but I do remember enough to get a human understanding that there certainly is life after death. It is very much like life on Earth but where the only emotion that exists is love. We are all an integral part of the whole. Each of us is that drop of water that is part of a bucket of water that is part of the whole ocean or source. Without each drop of water, the oceans would not exist. That is how important each of us is to the whole. The whole could not exist without each of us.

A favorite quote from my favorite poem is, ". . .No less than the trees and the stars; you have a right to be here." This is from the poem, *Desiderata*. I recommend that you read the entire poem; it is profound to say the least. If you look in the night sky, which star does not belong there? If you look at the trees in the forest, which tree does not belong there? The answer is obvious – every star and every tree belong exactly where they are. Just as you and every other human being belongs exactly on this Earth. You matter. We all matter.

Reincarnation

So exactly what is reincarnation? The general under-standing is that we live many lives or incarnations. So, why is it important to know this? I believe we carry the memories of past lives into our current life, and those memories can affect the way we live this current life.

Usually, the best and easiest way to understand your past lives is by undergoing hypnosis or hypnotherapy. With an experienced hypnotherapist, you can gain a better understanding of why you are the way you are and if these personality traits are affecting you positive-ly or negatively in this life. In my work, I have discov-ered that there are certain fears, phobias, and eccen-tric behaviors that people cannot quite seem to shake or understand even with traditional therapies. That is when clients typically come to me, when they have exhausted all other forms of healing and nothing has changed.

Shortly after a client sits down with me to talk about what they want to heal, I will typically see arrows shoot-ing over the top of their head, which is my indication the issue they want to address originates in a past life. I jokingly call these past life hangovers.

Here are a couple of examples: One young lady came to me wanting to address an eating disorder. In fact, she was anorexic. She had been to therapy, had tried various medications, and nothing seemed to work or last. When she began talking, I saw the arrow zipping over the top of her head and knew her issue had roots in a past life. I began asking her questions, such as was she overly concerned with expiration dates on food packages? Yes! Did she hate leftovers? Yes! Were there certain foods she absolutely would not touch that were normal to most people? Yes! After she answered those questions, I received images of a past life where she was starving to death and was forced to eat rancid food. She died of food poisoning in that life and happened to bring those memories into this life in the form of a fear of food, expressing itself as anorexia.

I created a release for her so she could, once and for all, eliminate the fear of food from this current life. Fifteen minutes after she left my office, she sent a text simply stating, "I ate!" That was two years ago, and to my knowledge, has not had an issue with food since.

Another lady came to me with an intense fear of heights. It was so bad that it was affecting her family life. What prompted her to make an appointment with me was that she was going on a trip to New York and knew she would be on a plane as well as was expected to go to the top of the Empire State Building. She did not think she was capable but did not want to ruin the trip for everyone else by her not participating. I saw the familiar arrows over her head and received information that in a past life she fell off the top of a mountain and was killed. She brought that fear, expressed as a fear of heights, into this life.

I created a release for her to eliminate her fear of heights and wished her well on her trip as she was leaving the next day. I also told her that, when she came for her next appointment, we were going to walk over a pedestrian bridge. The look on her face was priceless. It was a look that indicated she might not keep her next appointment.

A month later she showed up for her appointment, and I told her to keep her coat on because we were going for a drive to the nearest pedestrian bridge. She smiled and said, "Great!" Her fear had been so engrained the month before that I really thought I would have to hold her hand if I could get her to walk across the bridge at all. You can imagine my surprise when I saw the excitement on her face! We drove to the bridge; she jumped out of the car and began walking across the bridge by herself! At the apex of the bridge, she stopped and looked over the top at all the cars whizzing by us underneath the bridge. She smiled, laughed, and commented on how pretty it was to see the tops of the cars in the busy traffic below. We finished walking the bridge, and she asked if we could please do it again. Really!? Ok! And off we went.

I know these releases are incredibly powerful, but even I was surprised at her reaction. You see, there really are only two emotions: love and fear. If something is affecting you in a negative way, it is always fear based. Period. Once you eliminate the fear, you automatically eliminate the problem. The caveat to this is that the person must be willing to let go of the fear. Some people, unfortunately, find some kind of payday in hanging on to their fear or problem and really have no desire to heal. They might say they want to heal, but I can usually tell if the request is half-hearted or genuine.

So, what about the gifts we bring over with us from past lives? Most people do not give those a second thought since they are not affecting their current life in a negative way. Think about the things you do naturally – for fun. You take it for granted that you were just born that way. That part is true – you were just born that way. But almost always it is a skill or gift you have acquired by hard work in one or more past lives, and you decided to express that gift in a well-developed way in this lifetime.

I find that to be true with healers, for example. They know they have an innate ability to be a caregiver and want to help people, so they might choose to express their healing ability as a doctor, nurse, Reiki Master, Psychic medium, herbalist, expert in crystals, or even a personal trainer!

Another common trait I find with healers, especially those in the alternative healing fields such as psychic mediums, Reiki Masters, herbalists, tarot card readers, etc., is that they come in human form in this lifetime carrying over trauma from a past life. That trauma might be being accused of being a witch, being shunned or ostracized by their community, tortured, or even killed. It is no wonder they have energetic block after block in even claiming their gifts, let alone flourishing with their healing business!

I struggled with that very issue myself. I knew I was psychic from a fairly young age, but judgment from others kept me in fear. I was not able to claim that gift until I had undergone several hypnosis sessions and was a mature adult. Hypnosis revealed several things to me. The first was that I was an herbalist in one life and only cared about healing and caring for others by creating poultices, herb combinations, and teas to help the people in the village. My family in that lifetime, which also happens to be my family in this lifetime, turned on me. They held me down and killed me while the people in the village taunted them and me until I died. That fear of torture and death carried over into this life, expressing itself as a fear of being held down and an even bigger fear of claiming myself to be a healer.

One time I even had a spontaneous regression as I walked into an antique store. I walked up to a kneeling bench (which we never used in the religion in which I was raised) and, out loud, stated, "No wonder I have bad knees!" You see, I was born with congenital knee issues. There were misplaced tendons in both of my knees that kept pulling my kneecaps out of place, rendering me helpless and lying on the ground. The doctors said to wait until I was an adult before corrective surgery, so at 16 and 17 years of age, I had surgery on both of my knees six months apart. The kicker is that

I had surgery performed by a less than adequate surgeon, and now almost 50 years later, I still have knee issues.

At the time of this spontaneous regression in the antique store, however, I went back to the life of a nun who was constantly being punished by having to kneel and pray for hours on end. I distinctly remember thinking that, when I planned my current life, I decided no one would EVER make me kneel again! Well, I brought that promise into this lifetime with bad knees from birth that even surgery did not correct. To this day, I still cannot kneel. I did not even need hypnosis to figure that one out!

During another hypnosis session, I went back to that same life as a nun. What came up this time was that anyone in the clergy takes a vow of poverty. They know that the church will provide for them, but it is forbidden to have personal wealth. Well, let me tell you, that showed up in some interesting ways in this lifetime! As a child whenever I was given my allowance or made money from babysitting, I usually spent it the same day or within a day or two. It was as if I had an aversion to having money in my pocket. As I grew older and began my career, I barely made ends meet with some jobs. In other jobs, I made a particularly good living, better than most people but spent more than I earned and created huge amounts of debt. I was simply incapable of holding on to money. When I realized I had taken a vow of poverty in a past life, I did a release and, almost overnight, was able to begin to pay bills and even save! Such is the power of a past life hangover!

I believe we all have lived many lives – some of them on planet Earth and some elsewhere in the galaxy. When I ask people if they believe in past lives, many will say yes. Then I will ask them if they believe that some of those lives were lived on other planets other than Earth. I also believe that, in the lives lived here on Earth, we all have been every gender and every ethnicity. If that is true, why does racism exist? Why does sexism exist? We are basically prejudice against ourselves! How silly is that!?

I would encourage all of you to investigate a hypnosis session. You can discover and uncover more about who you really are and why you are here. It is so helpful if you have issues in your life that are holding you back from achieving what you want to achieve in this lifetime. You can get to the core of the issue, whether it began in this lifetime or any other lifetime. Wouldn't it feel great to eliminate the blocks that are keeping you from experiencing life to its fullest?

Many people have a fear of being hypnotized, thinking that someone else is controlling them. It is a fear of letting go. Nothing could be further from the truth. If you go to a reputable hypnotist or hypnotherapist, they will guide you, but it is YOU that is remembering past lives. No one can make you do anything that goes against your morals and values. There are stage hypnotists that, for entertainment value, will make people quack like a duck and do other silly things for pure entertainment value. Healing hypnosis is something quite different. For me, it is as if my brain has been split in two. One half of my brain is seeing what is unfolding from a past life or from my childhood in this life. The other half of my brain is the skeptical side – the side that thinks, "Wow, this is crazy! Where did this information come from?!" Every time I go under hypnosis it is like that, but I surrender to the process because I know it is helping me heal and live the best life I can.

Do you want to live your best life? What is holding you back? It is time to remember who you are – all of you!

Parallel Lives

If you now have a good understanding of source, soul, and spirit, let's take it another step further and talk about parallel lives.

This topic can be one of the hardest to wrap your head around, so just keep your mind open to the possibilities. It has been generally accepted that time does not exist. Clocks exist – time does not. Here on planet Earth, we created time to help us function in a linear way. The minute we leave planet Earth, such as when our souls leave our bodies at night or when we die, time no longer matters or exists. Everything happens at once. Confused already? Me too! As humans we are programmed to think in a linear way, so we really have no concept of what "no time" means.

When we think in the way of source, soul, and spirit, it can become a bit easier to understand. As we talked about in chapter 15, Source, Creator, God is all the same thing, correct? When we separate from source as separate souls, we become that bucket of water. We are still source, but we are now just a subset of source called a soul. That soul can split into many spirits, which are the drops of water, which are part of the bucket, which are part of the whole of source. Those spirits are living lives simultaneously. Most of us call them past lives. But if time does not exist, how can we have past lives or future lives, for that matter? We cannot. It is that simple. Ok, maybe it is not that simple, but it makes it a bit easier to understand.

A friend of mine had a husband who began complaining about a great deal of pain in his side. It would not go away. He went to several doctors who could find nothing wrong with him and kept sending him home. My friend went to see a local psychic and asked about her husband's pain. The psychic told my friend that, in a past life, which we now know is a parallel life, he was hit in the side (where the pain now resided) by a cannonball and subsequently died. The psychic told my friend to give that information to her husband. Both the psychic and my friend knew her husband would make fun of her for seeing a psychic as well as spending the money on such a stupid thing. The psychic said that it would not matter if he believed the story; his soul would recognize the information and the pain would be gone. My friend decided to risk it and went home and told her husband. As she suspected, her husband was angry at the money being spent and ridiculed her for wasting her time with a psychic. Here is the kicker. Her husband's pain was gone by the next morning and never came back. How do you explain that in human and medical terms? Because of parallel lives, the husband felt the pain at the same time it was happening to the other him – the other spirit expressing himself as a soldier in another lifetime, not a past life but a current life expressing itself differently.

In my personal experience, I would like to go back to my life as a nun. I could easily explain my knee pain by saying it came from my past life as a nun. In fact, that is how I usually do explain it rather than getting into the long discussion of explaining parallel lives. Most people accept the idea of past lives but still do not have a good understanding of them, so it is usually easier to explain current traumas by saying it is carried over from a past life.

So, back to my life as a nun, as I mentioned earlier. In the human form I am aware of now, I came into this existence with bad knees. My tendons were misplaced and used to pull my kneecaps out of place. This was very painful to say the least! The doctor who finally performed the surgery did not graduate at the top of his class. He was a bad doctor who really didn't do me any favors; and back in the mid-70's, physical therapy wasn't really a thing yet, so I have continued to have bad knees my entire life. So how does this fit into a parallel life? What has been made clear to me through meditation and hypnosis is that the nun life was so painful that, when the spirit that is now Kristi decided to express herself, she made the agreement that no one would ever make her kneel the way the spirit of the nun was forced to kneel. So, the life of a nun still exists with bad knees at the same time the life of Kristi still exists…with bad knees. This can happen because the nun and Kristi are different spirits, which are part of the same soul. That soul is part of the whole – the source.

I work with many parents who have lost children to ill-ness, accidents, and suicides. Obviously, this is incred-ibly painful for the parents and something they will have to learn how to incorporate into the rest of their own lives. The one comment expressed to me repeatedly is that the parent is afraid their child will have reincar-nated before the parent dies, therefore, the parent will never see their child again. Nothing could be further from the truth! If a child dies, their spirit will go back to the main soul. Other spirits from that same soul will be living other lives. When it comes time for the parent to pass away, the essence of their child will be there waiting for them. The essence is part of the original soul and cannot be destroyed. The parent will recog-nize their "child" immediately and they will be reunited as two souls on their way back to source.

Soul Mates and Twin Flames

So many people think their soul mate or twin flame must be a love relationship and/or an exclusive relationship. I personally do not think that is true. Let us break it down a bit and see if we can clarify exactly what is a soul mate and what is a twin flame.

What is a soul mate and how do you recognize yours? Firstly, I believe that we have many soul mates that enter our lives, representing different kinds of relationships. In my opinion, the first kind of soul mate is a soul partner and is an agreement with another soul. That agreement might be a relationship as a best friend, sibling, or business partner. They could be someone that you intimately know your entire life or someone you know for only a short period of time. It could be someone in your line of work who opens figurative doors for you, giving you a break of some kind. This is a specific agreement to help us professionally, emotionally, and spiritually.

Then there are romantic soul mates. These are the souls we are drawn to in quite a different way. Sometimes it is an instant recognition of that person's soul, but many times, it takes getting to know them before that certain "click" happens and our friendship energy shifts into something more emotional and physical. Just because they are a soul mate does not mean the relationship will last forever either. Remember, any kind of soul mate attraction is still an agreement between souls of what they want to help each other accomplish this time around in the human experience. That relationship can last forever or just a matter of a few minutes.

I believe any kind of soul mate relationship has ties to past lives, parallel lives, and life between lives. That is why our souls recognize this person. Our relationship with these people will certainly morph and change over time. When you do meet that romantic soul mate, many people will exclaim that they have never felt this way before or they have been waiting their whole life to meet them. There is a shift in their own soul and body when they meet the romantic soul mate.

Twin flames: I have a bit of a different opinion and experience in describing twin flames. Some people claim that twin flames are the same soul that split, and when they find each other, they are complete. I disagree with that to a certain extent. I believe twin flames are our greatest teachers. We come together to learn lessons and teach each other. Those lessons can, many times, be painful and abrasive towards the other person. That is why so many times you see twin flame relationships come together in a very intense way, split up and go their separate ways, get back together, split up, get back together – well, you get the idea. It is the proverbial love/hate relationship. You love them and cannot live without them, and then the conflict begins; and you cannot stand each other and decide to break up. After you've both cooled off for a bit and the dust has settled, you might reconnect, and the love begins again, only to repeat the cycle constantly. If you have been part of a relationship like that, the question is, "What am I supposed to learn from this person?" Do not play the victim! You are teaching them, and they are teaching you – you are not in this relationship to punish each other, although it might feel like it sometimes. You are in the relationship to teach each other and learn from each other.

I have also found with twin flames that the cycle does not necessarily have to repeat. You might learn the lessons you needed to learn the first time around. When you broke up, it was with the understanding that you learned from each other what you came here to learn, and that is enough!

When I do readings for people, one of the most frequently asked questions I get is – is he/she my soul mate? Is he/she "the one?" I always cringe just a little when that question is asked. Mostly, I have no business telling people whether to stay in a relationship or leave a relationship unless there is domestic violence involved. If that is the case – run! Find a safe person or place and run.

Most of the time the question is phrased, "Is he/she the one?" The way I want to answer is that if you must ask me, then no, he is or she is not the one. Although that is what I want to say, I rarely do because that would just be rude. The way I typically answer that question is this way: most romantic relationships need to unfold naturally. If I were to tell you that yes, he is the one, you will be out shopping for a wedding dress tomorrow. If I tell you that no, he is not the one, you will want to break up with the poor guy because you will feel like you are wasting your time and want to make space for the real right one.

I emphasize that each relationship is a lesson we agreed to before we were born, and that relationship needs to run its course. You will intrinsically know when it is time to walk away or tie the knot. You do not need a psychic to tell you that. Follow your gut instinct or your intuition, and let them be your guides. There is a gift in everything, even in so-called failed relationships. What did you learn from that person? That relationship? Most of the time, what we learn is what we do not want! That is a powerful lesson for sure! With each relationship we fine-tune what serves us best for our soul growth.

Ok, I can hear many of you out there screaming at me. Yea, but what if he left me? I did not do anything! Well,

I am sorry to tell you this, but there is no innocent party in a relationship. A relationship is always a two-way street. Yes, you are hurt. Yes, you are devastated. Yes, you have been betrayed. Yes, you are lost. But you must examine your role in the relationship. You did play a part, but what part did you play? The victim? The ostrich with your head buried in the sand? The control freak? The partner who neglected the other one because you were too busy caring for the children? The non-communicator?

Trust me, you did play a part in all relationships in your life. Perhaps now is the time to examine what part you did play. More importantly, do you want to repeat that role in your next relationship? Ouch, I know. I feel your pain. It is always hard to point the finger at yourself. Look for the gift. What did you learn from that soul mate, that twin flame? Did you learn what you need from a relationship? Did you learn what you do not want in a relationship? Did you learn a bit more about your strengths or your points of vulnerability? That is what relationships are! To continue to learn who we are! We are just learning those lessons with the help of another soul who was brave enough to take on these joyful and, sometimes, painful lessons. If you create our own reality, you must learn what part you play in all relationships. These lessons come from both your soul mates, your twin flame, and every other member of your soul group.

So, what is a soul group? We talked about this in Chapter 14. A soul group is a group of souls with which we are intimately connected. We reincarnate with them over and over again. We work with these souls in between lives to plan what our next life will look like, the lessons we want to learn, and the things we want to experience. We work with these souls to determine what part they will play in our next life and what part we will play in theirs. Just like in theater production, we agree to play certain parts. Yes, sometimes we agree to play the bad guy, or someone we love in spirit form agrees to play the bad guy so we can experience and learn what we want to. In the next life we might really hate this person – the bad guy – but the minute we return to spirit, we recognize that soul and what they did to help the evolution of our soul, even if we hated them for a good portion of our human life.

It really is much easier to understand when you think in terms of a theater production or movie. There are actors playing parts. The minute the curtain comes down or the director yells cut, we shed the character of the part we were playing and resume being ourselves. So does every other character in the play or movie. We hug, congratulate each other on a great performance, which includes the good guys and the bad guys. It is all an act where none of it is real. That is exactly what it is here on Earth. It is all an act to allow us to progress and evolve as souls, experiencing the joys of life as well as the hard things in life too. We are all characters playing different parts and wearing different costumes each time we reincarnate.

We have our intimate soul group, and then we have souls that are on the fringe of our group. Those are the souls that might show up briefly in our lives to provide compassion when we especially need it, or they might be the mean boss, teacher, or co-worker that we know for a short amount of time but make a huge impact on our lives and move us forward in our soul progression.

When we leave this life, we will recognize them and thank them for the part they played, and in return, they will thank us. Even those souls who are the hardest to love during a lifetime are usually the souls that love us the most and are, therefore, willing to play the hardest part. We do it for the love of each other.

Talking to the Dead

Many people can at least sense when the deceased are around them, especially if it is a family member or loved one. People are also quick to claim they made it all up. I am here to tell you that is not true. What you sense or feel is true and real. The veil is thinning between this world and the other side, and more and more people are becoming aware of the energies that lay beyond our five senses. It is also becoming more acceptable to talk about our experiences, which is huge in the effort to have metaphysics and medium work be mainstream. This is how many people begin the conversation when they come to see me for an appointment: "You're going to think I'm crazy, but..." I usually know exactly what they are going to say. They are going to tell me that they saw someone, smelled something that reminded them of their grandmother, or felt someone brush their neck. Trust it – it is true!

Here is how I communicate with the deceased: since I am mostly clairvoyant, the deceased send me pictures. These pictures are not seen with my eyes; they are seen in my head. When someone is sitting across from me for an appointment, the first thing I do is look around my client to see if there are any shadows or shifts in energy. I rarely see a person standing there; it is usually a shadow or silhouette but, more importantly, it is where the shadow is standing that helps me determine how they are connected to my client. If I see a shadow at my client's right shoulder, I know their mother or a mother figure has passed. If the shadow is at the left shoulder, I know the father or father figure has passed. If the shadow is behind the shoulder, I know it is a grandmother or grandfather. If the shadow is in front of the shoulder, I know the client has lost a child. If the shadow is directly in front of the client, I know it is a friend or sibling.

Here is where it gets interesting – If a shadow comes in and will not look at me and will only look at the client, I know the deceased person takes some responsibility for their own passing. This usually means alcoholism, drug addiction, overeating, smoking, or generally not taking care of themselves when they really knew better.

If a deceased person comes in backwards and hunched over, I know it is a suicide.

Once I have identified who the deceased loved one is and what their relationship is to my client, the "shadow" starts sending me pictures. Those pictures usually begin in the form of energy and generally describe their personality and things they might have struggled with in this life. This is providing validation to the client that I have the right person. Once we have validated that I have identified the correct person, the deceased loved one begins sending me more detailed pictures. The trick is translating the pictures. I will tell you the deceased have a funny sense of humor! They will send me pictures that have me laughing while my client is beginning to wonder if I am the one that is crazy!

Translating those pictures can be tricky indeed. Through the years I have developed certain symbols, which are the same for any client and from any spirit. For instance, if a loved one pops through carrying a cake, I know there is a birthday or anniversary that has passed in the last ten days or is coming up in the next 10 days. If a loved one comes through carrying a baby blanket, I know either my client or the deceased loved one has had a miscarriage, still birth, or abortion. If the blanket is white, there is no identifiable gender. Otherwise, it is shown to me as either pink or blue.

If you are starting to see, hear, or sense things, just say hello! Maybe I should clarify… if you recognize the energy as belonging to a loved one, then say hello. If the energy feels off somehow or makes you uncomfortable in any way, you have the right to tell them to leave.

When I first went public as a psychic medium, I was insecure about messages I was getting, and I was very afraid to be wrong. The best piece of advice I ever received was that spirit never lets you down. I interpreted that in a few ways:

1) I needed to trust that spirit would come through.

2) I did not need to wait for spirit to come through; I could ask them! This was huge for me. I was so used to waiting for spirit to come through that it made me nervous and insecure that they might not come through.

3) I could have conversations with spirit! I could ask them how they passed and how long they have been gone. I could ask them to give me a random detail of some kind that I could not possibly know about them or my client. To me, the more random the message, the better. You cannot make this stuff up!

Spirit wants to come though and bring peace and closure to the loved ones left behind. The message I almost always get is that the other side of heaven is beautiful! The spirits are healthy and happy and want the ones left behind to move on, heal, and live a healthy life here on Earth. Nothing makes deceased loved ones happier than to see the ones left behind flourishing and living out their dreams…fearlessly.

When I begin a session with a client, I always give the speech or description of how I work. Mostly, this is so the client has an idea of what to expect. I start by explaining that as a medium I can connect with those on the other side, but it is always up to them, not me, whether they can show up. The deceased must learn how to lower their vibration while I raise mine and, hopefully, we meet in the middle. They run the show; I do not! I also explain that the information I get is correct, but it is whether I can correctly translate the pictures they are sending me. It is very much like charades! That is why I like my sessions to be conversational. We can validate and clarify to make sure I am doing my job and translating the pictures correctly.

The day after my mother passed away, I was driving 3 hours to my home in Omaha. I needed to clear my head, pack some clothes for her funeral, and head back to Sioux Falls. During the drive, I felt my mother's energy pop in my car. I was startled and told her I knew she would come to me, however, I did not think it would be so soon. I asked her if she was ok. Since she passed from cancer and really struggled with breathing the last few weeks of her life, I needed to know if she was free from that struggle. She smiled, pounded her chest like a gorilla, and took the biggest and deepest breath I am sure she had taken in many years.

I laughed, knowing she would make the best of the situation, but also told her how sorry I was that she had to go through what she did. She just shrugged and said that it was nothing. I told her it might be nothing now, but she certainly had a rough time of it when she was here and, for that, I was sorry. Here is the profound thing she said next. She said, "Kristi, it is so much harder being born than dying." When she said that, I could barely keep my car on the freeway. Her words hit me like no other words I had ever heard in my life. Think about it – when we come into this world, it is not only the process of being born but it is coming into a world where we have plans, roadblocks, setbacks, and heaven only knows what else. Our future is uncertain coming into this human body. When we die, we are really going home – our true home. How beautiful is that?

On some occasions, I will tune into people who are still alive but are either close to transitioning or are in a place where they are unable to communicate with their loved ones.

Here is an example: One day on a cold February morning, I received a phone call that my father had had a major stroke. He was living in Arizona at the time, so I made my plane reservations to immediately fly down to see him. While I was waiting for the right time to leave for the airport, I decided to call a friend of mine just to have someone to talk to since my dad was not expected to live through the night.

While I was on the phone with my friend, my dad popped in my living room. I told my friend what I was seeing, and she was kind enough to ask me questions. She asked what he was wearing. I told her blue jeans, a white t-shirt, and a cap. She then asked why he was there. I told her he was deciding whether to live or to die. She asked what he had decided. I said he has decided to die but he is going to wait until March. About the time my dad disappeared, we finished our conversation, and I left to go catch my flight.

I met some of my siblings at the airport in Phoenix, and then we all went to the ICU to see our dad. He was awake and recognized his kids right away, emitting the biggest smile on his face. From that moment on, he increasingly improved until the nursing staff said they had no idea why he was still here and that were moving him to a regular room rather than ICU. My siblings and I had been at the hospital for several days when he was moved to a regular room, so we decided he was going to be fine and made plans to fly back to our respective homes. I got home that night and went to bed early since the stress of the last few days had really gotten to me. Around midnight that night, my brother called telling me that dad had passed away just a few minutes before. The date was March 3rd. He knew exactly when he was going to pass, and he came to tell me about a week ahead of time.

Another time I was able to tune in to someone who was still living was when I was doing an audience reading and was drawn to a particular lady. Her son was coming through to me, but I could tell by where he showed up that he was still alive and not deceased. To protect her privacy, I cannot name names, but I can tell you her son came through loud and clear to me, expressing that I was to tell his mother he was still alive. He had been abducted many years before and had been unable to communicate with his mother in human form, so he chose to come through me and get the message to his mother.

Another way living people come through to me is when they have dementia or Alzheimer's. They appear to me as deceased, but when my clients claim their loved one is still alive, I ask if they have dementia or Alzheimer's. The answer is always yes. You see, when people have these diseases, they frequently leave their body. That is why you find them napping more often the deeper into the disease they are. They frequently leave their body and check out the astral plane until it is truly their time to pass.

If you are beginning to see dead people and are not sure what is going on or how to interpret what you are seeing, hearing, or sensing, practice, practice, and practice until the signs, symbols and energies are recognizable to you. You can also just ask the spirit that comes through – are you in your body our out of your body? They will answer you correctly, which will then lead you to your next set of questions. If they are in their body, you might ask them why they are coming through to you. Do you need to get a message to a loved one? Are they in danger? What message do they want you to deliver? If they are out of body, you might ask them how they passed. They will almost always answer your questions. If they do not answer directly, it is usually because they do not want to tell you or it is not important to the session.

Suicide and Murder

In the metaphysical world, there are differing opinions and much controversy. Suicide and murder can be one of the most controversial. What I am stating in this chapter comes from my own studies and talking to people on the other side who have been murdered or committed suicide. There are many in my community, let alone the world, who might disagree with me, and that is their right. I always say that if someone claims to know it all – they are wrong – period. No one knows it all on this side of the veil or even the other side of the veil. Therefore, I need to state upfront that what I am writing here comes from my own experiences, which may vary vastly from your own.

Let us begin with suicide. What I have been told is that suicide is a choice – that is all – a choice. There is no stigma attached to it; there is no judgment, except from the spirit themselves towards their own decision. There is no eternity in Hell either. These are all archaic notions that no longer serve a purpose in modern life.

There is not a week that goes by in which I do not read for someone who has lost a loved one to suicide. It is heartbreaking and tragic to see the pain in the souls of those left behind. Believe me, it is so much harder on those still here in the physical world than it is for the one who took his or her own life. The messages obviously vary from reading to reading, but one of the constant themes is that the person who took their life did not realize the value their life had to others; they did not realize the impact their life had on others. I am not just talking family members. I am talking about friends, friends of friends, and relatives of friends of friends. I equate it to skipping a rock on a lake. The ripples continue as far as the eye can see. That is the impact one soul has on the planet. Another way to look at it is by envisioning a tapestry, a beautiful and intricately woven piece of art. We have all seen what happens when one thread is pulled in a snag or one piece of thread is removed completely. It can ruin the entire piece. Each piece of thread and color is important to the whole. The art will never be the same. A new piece of thread can be added, but it still makes the piece different from the original. It is the same with human souls on the planet. Each one is here for a specific reason; each one is part of the whole. Each one has a right to be here and deserves to be here.

When souls who have taken their own lives come through to me from the other side, they usually come through with great humility because it took taking their own lives to really understand how important they were (are) to the whole of humanity. In human form, their world usually gets smaller and smaller as they draw into themselves. I am talking about emotionally getting smaller and smaller. They may still appear to the outside world as fun and gregarious, but inside, they are losing themselves. This could be because of depression, mental illness, addiction, neglect, or abuse. The reasons really do not matter. What does matter is that this soul did not feel valued, did not feel heard, did not feel understood.

Was it up to those left behind to carry the pain? Not necessarily. Many times, those left behind were completely unaware of the pain their loved one was in. Other times they were perfectly aware and did everything they could, but nothing seemed to work. There really is no one to blame. How can I say that?! What does that really mean?

With everything I have read and studied in more than 40 years, most of the time it is an agreement between the loved ones left behind and the soul who took their own life. In spirit form, one soul agreed to reach a certain age or let certain circumstances dictate that they would commit suicide. Another soul stepped up and said they wanted to experience what it was like to be the one left behind, to pick up the pieces when a loved one took their own life. You see? It is almost always an agreement between souls to help them learn the lessons they wanted to learn, experience what they wanted to experience, and accomplish what they wanted to accomplish. I have to say, this is one of the hardest concepts for people to understand. The response I usually hear is, "I would NEVER choose this experience!" In human form, they are right, no one would ever consciously choose to have that kind of pain inflicted on themselves. But we are not talking about humans making this agreement. We are talking about spirit making this agreement, and spirit is energy. Energy never dies; it just changes form. So, as humans we think of our loved ones as dead and that we will never see them again. But in spirit, we know they are not dead; they are energy that has just changed form.

I believe that, when we come into this human existence, we come with an end date and an end way in mind. In other words, a soul might only live a few days, weeks, or months. They might decide that they want to live to 100. That choice was made in spirit form before they were ever born. They also choose an end way, meaning that the spirit might choose to die of cancer, a heart attack, or some other disease. They might also choose their exit by having an accident or being murdered. They might also decide to end their own life at a certain age in a certain way.

Another message I have received frequently is that, when a person decides to take their own life, it might not have been pre-planned. After all, we do live on a planet of free will. When we are planning our lives, as

I have mentioned before, we set ourselves up to learn lessons, accomplish and experience things. When we get here, however, things might be a bit more difficult than we anticipated. So, during the planning phase, we also insert, what I call, early outs. An early out is an opportunity for us to exit this life without completing our original plan. That can end up being a freak accident, a murder, or most common, a suicide or a drug over-dose. Life can feel too much for them to handle. I like to say that they bit off more than they could chew. Rather than struggle the rest of their lives, many spirits decide to take their own life, knowing they will have to come back and do it all over again. Hopefully, in their next life, they will plan differently, and in a way, that is a bit easier for them to handle.

When a soul makes that decision to take their life, there really is no judgment from the other side. Your loved one is safe, happy, and at peace. A soul does judge themselves, usually for the pain they left behind for their friends and family. I just want to be clear that your deceased loved ones are at peace no matter how they chose to leave their life.

Let us move on to murder, which can be even more of a sensitive topic than suicide. My belief is that no one can die without their permission. Yes, you read that correctly. No one can die without their permission, and that also means being murdered.

Here's where things get interesting and controversial. If we are here to learn lessons and experience things, we must understand that some spirits have chosen to experience being murdered. Their life is never taken or ended by a so-called enemy, although it may appear that way to those left behind. It is my understanding that a spirit who chooses the experience of being mur-dered cannot do it alone – they need another soul to agree to help them. A soul, usually very well connected to them in spirit form, agrees to help them experience being murdered. That soul says, "I love you so much, I'm willing to do this for you." The soul who agrees to be the murderer also wants to experience what it is like to murder someone. The two souls agree long before either of the spirits have been born.

I want to be truly clear on one thing: just because two souls agree on this does not mean the murderer should not be caught, punished, and removed from society. They need to spend the rest of their lives in prison. The spirit who has agreed to be the murderer, many times, has planned to live a life of trauma, abuse, and pain so they can be in the frame of mind to take another's life. Rarely does a murder happen by someone who is healthy, balanced, and grounded. As we all know, most murders are committed by a person who has led a life of pain, whether it is obvious to others or not. They have set themselves up to this kind of life which makes it more conducive not to value human life and therefore be able to take someone else's life. That spirit wanted to experience what it was like not to value human life, live a troubled life, and spend time in prison with other people who hold similar values.

Just like when you go to the theater to see a play or a movie, there is the good guy and the bad guy. The audience hates the bad guy because that is what the writer, director, and actors intended. When the curtain goes down, the actors hug and shake each other's hands, congratulating each other on a great performance! They all know it was an act – a part each person agreed to play. It is no different in life. Each spirit agrees to play a part until the spirit decides to leave the body. At that point, after both have passed on, they greet each other with gratitude and love for helping the other live the life they chose and experience what they wanted to experience.

I understand it is hard to wrap your head around this concept, but I have had enough spirits come through in sessions to confirm what I have stated here. If we live many, many lives, the life of being murdered or being the murderer is just a blip on the screen of life. The real pain goes to those left behind. Here is the kicker – those left behind have also agreed on a soul level to BE the ones left behind so they can experience the pain of losing someone they love in such a horrific way. The lives we choose to live are woven in an intricate tapestry in conjunction with other souls.

I also want to state that the things I talk about here are coming from my experiences as a psychic medium and my conversations with the other side. I cannot state for certain that this is what life is all about. Again, if anyone tells you they know what is best or what is right, they are wrong. No one knows for sure – no one – until we are on the other side ourselves. We can all only follow our own paths in the way that feels best to us. There are no mistakes. Trust that you are living your life perfectly. The question is, are you the person you want to be? Are you living the life you want to live? There is no wrong way to live life. There is only what makes you happy, whole, and peaceful. If you do not feel happy, it is always up to you, and only you, to change. All change begins on the inside. The inside of you. Only you can control you. When you blame other people, you are giving away your power. Claim who you are and who you want to be. How do you become resilient after the tragedy of losing someone to suicide or murder? It is always inside of you to choose. Know that you deserve a joyful and happy life even in the face of unspeakable loss.

What Do We Do on the other side

It has been my experience that what our loved ones do on the other side very much corresponds either with what they did when they were in human form or what they wished they did in human form. For instance, I have had deceased souls come through to me telling me that they are working with children on the other side. It might be that they are teachers or are there to help young souls cross over, in other words, acting like a bit of a greeter to make a young person's transition easier. Some other occupations I have been shown are that of a dancer, a bartender, someone who helps souls evolve by helping them plan their next life. I have even had someone come through who was an influencer to loved ones left behind, helping them heal.

When my friend Mike passed away and he came to visit and show me the other side, I asked what he was doing. In human form, Mike always wanted to be in law enforcement of some kind. He never had the courage to pursue that line of work and stayed doing the work he knew he was good at instead of pursuing where his heart wanted him to go. On the other side, when I asked him what he did now that he was dead, he just kind of laughed at me and said he was studying. I asked what he was studying, and he said justice, which is certainly a form of law enforcement. There was much more that he was studying, but it was too much for me to understand from a human perspective.

Suffice it to say that, when we cross over to the other side, we still have "jobs," although maybe not in the traditional sense. We still have responsibilities, which include jobs as well as interactions with other souls. I was raised to believe that, when we die, we go to Heaven and sit on a cloud like a cherub and maybe play a harp. I never wanted to die because I thought that would be the most boring existence ever! Who would want to just sit around all day?! Well, I assure you that is not what we do. That is not to say we cannot just sit around or do the things we loved to do as humans. I have had the deceased come through riding motorcycles, fixing cars, drinking beer, cooking food – even smoking! These are things they loved to do when they were on this side of the veil, so they continue to do those things on the other side too. The benefit is there is no cancer, alcoholism, obesity, or the other habits that cause harm to the human body because they no longer HAVE a human body!

I have communicated with a great deal of parents and grandparents who are taking care of babies. Typically, these babies are little souls that are waiting to be born. Often, these little souls come through to me as a miscarriage, abortion, or still birth first. The agreement with the parent is that this little soul wanted to experience what it was like to live only a few weeks – and that includes being in utero. That little soul might say that is all they wanted to experience, period or, more likely, what they wanted to experience at that time and will come though the same parents later when they are ready to live longer. As I mentioned before, we come into this human existence with an end date and an end way in mind. Many times, the end way is a miscarriage, abortion, or still birth. Sometimes it is a baby who might die of SIDS. That is simply what they chose to experience in this lifetime. Remember, we are all energy and energy does not die – it just changes form. That little spirit of energy will most likely come back in another human body, only this time, choosing to live longer. Let me assure you that no soul leaves their body before they are ready or in a way not of their choosing.

I know this is difficult to understand, let alone wrap your head around, but it is true. I meet with grieving family members every day who believe the way their loved one died could not possibly be what they intended. I understand how they think that way. It is so hard to comprehend why anyone would agree to being murdered, abused, neglected, or ending their life in any way that involves violence of any kind.

When we die, no matter our occupation or experiences on Earth, we return to a place of love. In that place of love, we can do anything or be anything we choose. That is why the first time I heard the phrase "all men are created equal" I did not understand. Really? If we are created equal, why do some people thrive, and others do not? Why do some people come into this world with the deck stacked against them? Well, now after communicating with so many deceased people, I have a better understanding of what the phrase means. We ARE all CREATED equal. We all have the same opportunity to come into human form and experience whatever we choose. Our souls are created equal. Our souls can experience whatever they choose while here on Earth in human form. When we leave this human body, we go back to our original spirit form to share what we learned. The more we experience, whether it be here on Earth or on another planet, it is helping our soul evolve.

One of my favorite things to tune into are spirit guides. That too is an occupation on the other side! Spirit guides have lived many, many lives and are thereby qualified to help us live our lives. They understand how difficult being human can be, so they have chosen to help us navigate the lives we have chosen to live this time around. What many people do not understand is that, by being a spirit guide for us, we are helping them evolve as a soul too! Next time around, they might incarnate as human with us agreeing to be spirit guides for them. Both souls learn. Both souls evolve. This side and the other side. It is a beautiful matrix.

out of Body Experiences/Astral Travel

We have all had out of body experiences, but many of us do not remember them. Let us begin with the out of body experiences that we read about in books or hear through stories. To put it simply, an out of body experience is when soul leaves the physical body. Unless you die, the soul always returns to the physical body.

So why would the soul leave the body? Our real home is out of the body, so it is very natural and common for the soul to go home – even if it is just for a moment.

Many have heard or are aware of the silver cord. This is the cord that attaches the soul to the physical body. When that cord is severed, we transition or die. If that cord is not severed during an out of body experience, the soul will always return to the body. I have had several out of body experiences during meditation or once during a rare afternoon nap. I awoke from this nap, and my soul was hovering about two to three inches above my body. I was completely aware, a bit freaked out, and not quite sure what to do! I decided to calmly ask my soul to rejoin my body. Poof, in the blink of an eye, I was back in my body. Evidently, my soul had been out gallivanting and was not quite ready for me to wake up.

I have heard numerous accounts of people leaving their body during surgery. In recovery, they can report exactly what happened, what the surgeon was doing as well as the other nurses during the surgery. Doctors and nurses are usually astounded to hear the exact details that no one could possibly know unless they were hovering above the operating table and observing everything.

Another common way to experience an out of body experience is through an accident of some kind. These examples are different from a near death experience, however. In a near death experience, it is witnessed and determined that the individual's heartbeat has stopped and no pulse is found. The dead person goes through a tunnel, meets God or the deity of their belief system, is told it is not their time, and are sent back to Earth. An out of body experience is very different. The person does not die. The soul simply hovers over their body until it is time to reenter the body.

Sometimes, in addition to hovering, the soul will astral travel to other parts of the cosmos. There are countless witnesses who, usually during a tragic event, have strong memories of leaving their body. They are aware of paramedics working on them at an accident or even of doctors performing surgery. Most are aware of seeing the silver cord connecting the soul to the body. They can articulate in amazing detail what happened while they were being attended to by paramedics or doctors.

Now, let us talk about the rest of us having out of body experiences but not remembering them. We all astral travel or have out of body experiences every night when we sleep. The body needs rest; the soul does not. While our bodies are resting at night, our souls leave the body and do other things. What other things, you might ask? Well, that just depends. The soul can meet up with other members of their soul group while they too are having out of body experiences. The soul can also travel to other dimensions where it does work, learns, or enjoys being "home."

Do you ever wake up in the morning knowing something happened but are not able to quite define what it was? Do you ever have those moments while you are sleeping where you are suddenly jolted awake for no reason? Your body jumps? That is your soul returning to your body! You have been out wandering in the cosmos, and your soul decided to come back to the physical body. We do not always feel the jolt of returning to the body, but many times we do. We suddenly become wide awake and wonder if someone is breaking into our home since the jolt we felt was so jarring. But if you also will notice, even though the jolt is jarring, you usually can fall back to sleep in a matter of minutes. Feeling that sensation is very natural, and astral traveling is something the body is used to doing. Our soul usually does it gracefully to where we do not even notice it. Other times, it comes screaming back to the body like it has a deadline to meet!

Whether it is an out of body experience or your soul is astral traveling, there is no need for alarm. Both events are very natural to the body, and we do them frequently – we just rarely remember them.

Many people take lessons in astral traveling and can leave the body at will. Although I find it fascinating, I am perfectly content knowing I leave my body most every night, but I have little desire to do it consciously. If this is something you want to do, you must be very comfortable with a consistent meditation routine. All purposeful astral traveling events begin with meditation. It takes practice, determination, and tenacity to achieve at-will astral traveling. I will say that, while leaving the body, I have had many incredible experiences communicating with my guides on the other side. One time, I was hesitating on whether to enter a romantic relationship. I asked the question of my guides before I went to sleep that night. During the night, I met my guides on the astral plane, and they showed me at a casino gambling. For anybody who knows me, they know I am not a gambler, so this message was clear to me that entering this relationship would be a big gamble. My guides also showed me two friends of mine who were in a relationship that always had me puzzled. The male was so dominant; the female was very submissive. I knew I could never be in a relationship such as that one. When my guides showed me the couple, it became noticeably clear that the choice was still mine, but I would be getting involved in a relationship that did not suit me at all. I woke up, back in my body, and started laughing. My guides took me on a little trip, and what they showed me made the decision abundantly clear to not get involved.

Near Death Experiences

The term near death experience, or NDE, was first popularized by Dr. Raymond Moody in his book *Life After Life*. If you have not read this book, I highly recommend it.

A near death experience is hard to describe or explain because no human words seem adequate to define it. I will do the best I can to explain based on my own experiences as well as the help from others who have had experiences.

An NDE is a life-changing experience associated with death or an impending death that share similar characteristics. A couple of my favorite books on the topic are Life After Life as I mentioned earlier, *Proof of Heaven* by Dr. Eben Alexander, and *Dying to Be Me* by Anita Moorjani. I have read and reread these books many times as they attempt to portray life on the other side. My own experience was quite a bit different from these authors but a near death experience, nonetheless.

It is my understanding that an NDE begins with someone who has died during an accident, surgery, or other life-altering event. Generally, the person's soul leaves their body and floats above, observing or trying to figure out what has happened to them! There is always a sense of peace, never panic or fear. Many times, the soul is drawn to a light, which presents itself as a tunnel of beautiful white light. The dying person is inextricably drawn to the light. This light is so bright that it would be blinding while still in the human body but seems to be bright, but magnetic, while out of the body.

Going through this tunnel of white light, many souls will see deceased loved ones or spirit guides. Their senses are heightened, and there also seems to be an altered perception of time. Once on the other side of the tunnel of light, they often will come upon an unearthly environment and will see colors, shapes, and other things that do not exist on Earth but are so beautiful they defy description. That is what makes it so difficult to share an experience once back in the human body. There truly are no words or pictures to define or describe what they have seen.

Many souls report having a life review. A life review is described as judgment day by those who have never had an NDE. For those of us who have had a life review, let me tell you – it is vastly different from what anyone expects! Judgment day comes with the connotation that someone else is judging you, pointing out all your sins, shortcomings, and faults. This could not be further from the truth!

At some point in an NDE, there is a border or a point of no return. This is when the soul is met by loved ones, guides, angels, or religious figures, telling this soul that it is not their time and that they must return to Earth. If they were to cross the border, they would not be able to return to human life and would permanently stay on the other side. I've yet to meet anyone who has experienced an NDE who wanted to come back to human life. Human life on Earth is hard! Many times, people come back to Earth because they are told and shown that their work on Earth is not finished. There are still things for them to do. They begrudgingly return to Earth, knowing that one day they will again leave their body, go through the process again, and, only this time, will not return.

How long does an average (if there is such a thing!) NDE last? It has been reported that they last anywhere from a few to several minutes. This does not seem like a long time for the mentioned things to happen, but with that altered perception of time, many things can happen in what feels like a short amount of time.

When someone does return from an NDE, they never have a fear of death again. They have seen how beautiful and peaceful it is, and they also know there are loved ones, angels, and guides waiting for them. They are powerfully transformed as human beings in ways not to be described other than they are more sensitive to beauty, and they find beauty in many more things. They also now recognize how many people live in fear and hate. They can no longer tolerate what we would call normal human emotions. They have a greater appreciation of life, higher self-esteem, as well as greater compassion for others. They also can return with a greater purpose and drive for spirituality, love, and care for our environment, as well as other planetary concerns.

I do know some people return and then experience depression. Almost always, that depression is a result of not being able to share their experience with others for fear of being judged or knowing they will not be able to adequately explain what has happened. I am asking that, if you know someone who has had an NDE, please keep an open mind, ask questions, and most of all – listen and believe them!

Here is my own experience: it is not an NDE in the traditional sense. I was five years old and extremely sick with a case of the flu that would not end. My whole family had this flu and recovered in a few short days. My flu continued until, on the 5th day, my mother finally called the doctor who told her to get me to the hospital as quickly as she could. When we arrived at the hospital, I was put in a bed filled with ice to lower my temperature and was also fed a cold orange soda. Sometime during the night, I was visited by beings from another planet. Now, I know you are thinking I was hallucinating and, on one level I cannot disagree, but this event has shown up many times in hypnosis as a real event and not a hallucination. I was told by these beings that I would always be safe and protected. I did not question it or even repeat it to my family or the doctor as it seemed a logical thing to be told to a five-year-old little girl. If I did tell anyone, I am sure I probably said that the doctor told me I would always be safe and protected. Who would even question that?

How is this an NDE, you might ask? I did almost die as the doctor told my parents the next day. I did not go to the light, but it was as if the light came to me instead. You see, when one of the beings entered my room, there was a light so bright I could barely see. This was in the middle of the night when there were no lights on in my hospital room and no ambient light of any kind.

I do know that, after that event, I put the safe and protected statement to the test many times, living a life of a confused child and then a troubled teen. This continued into adulthood until I was introduced to metaphysics. Little by little, my life changed, albeit with many setbacks. Finally, one night I was taken to the other side where I met my council of elders and had a life review.

A council of elders is different from spirit guides in a few ways; the council helps you plan your many lives whereas spirit guides help you achieve what you came into this life to achieve. Your council of elders is yours alone. They do work closely with your spirit guides to help you live your best life…if you choose.

Your council of elders is usually made of spirits who are vibrating at an extremely high level. Whereas, when we are in human form, we vibrate at a relatively low level, so we do not overwhelm the physical body.

As humans, we also vibrate at a low level, so we can have the human experience, which, in essence, means accomplishing our life lessons while blindfolded. By blindfolded, I mean we come here on Earth with little to no memory of who we really are in spirit form. I think it would defeat the purpose if we remembered every-thing! What fun is learning lessons if we already know them?!

Life Review and Judgment

A huge part of my job is to connect with people's deceased loved ones. One of the things I love most about doing this is that there is nothing but love on the other side. People come to me for mediumship for various reasons. Sometimes, it is because of unfinished business or loneliness or because they miss their deceased loved one. Other times, it is due to guilt because they did not get to say goodbye. Many times, however, it is because the person dying feared death and hung on as long as they could before the body finally gave out and their loved one left behind wants to connect and make sure they are happy, at peace, or holding no grudges.

I also deal with countless suicides and drug overdoses. The surviving family members or friends come to me to make sure their loved one is in Heaven and that they are ok. Because of religious beliefs, I find that so many people are not only afraid to die but are more afraid of living. They have been taught that if they do not believe or if they behave in certain ways, they will be judged and sent to Hell. I am here to tell you that is not true.

Now, do not get me wrong! I think religions can be beautiful. They can uplift, center, and ground people. That is not what this chapter is about. It is when mankind got ahold of religion that things began to look different. Religion is about your personal relationship with God. God does not care whether you believe or not – God just is. God does not care whether you behave in this life – God wants you to be happy. God wants you to experience what you came here to experience.

When I was 17 years old and at my high school graduation party, I announced that I was an atheist. You can guess that didn't go over well with my parents and my Lutheran upbringing. I could not understand why, if

God is all loving, we should fear him. All the pictures I was ever shown of God were of some old man looking simply pissed off at me and the entire human race. I would ask my parents questions. I asked the Lutheran youth minister questions that no one could answer to my satisfaction. What I did not realize was that I was not an atheist – I was agnostic. I was questioning the existence of God and what that meant to me and the rest of the world. I knew at that point that there were certainly other religions that taught different theologies.

My family even had a family friend stay with us who said she had to go to Catholic mass or she would end up going to hell. My whole family went to a Catholic mass to save this poor girl's soul from eternal damnation. My question was why weren't we, my family, going to hell for missing our Lutheran service that Sunday? I was basically told to shut up and go with it. No more questions. The thing is, this girl made me feel less than because I was not Catholic. So, which religion was right? Did I need to convert to Catholicism? As I grew older, I began studying other religions, not seriously but enough to grasp the basic concept. Some religions, I discovered, did not even believe in God! Hmm, maybe I was on the right path claiming myself as atheist! It was all so confusing to this teenage version of myself.

Religion is one of those things that is so programmed into most of us (lucky are those who are not programmed!) that we can spend a lifetime trying to make sense of it all, reconciling ourselves to what we really believe against what we have been programmed to believe.

Fear is an unbelievably powerful tool. It begins with our parents telling us we must behave in a certain way… or else. Most parents do this with the intent of teaching us social mores, morals, and values. The intent is good, but it is coming from people's own programming.

The programming continues with teachers in school, friends, other family members, co-workers, and bosses, let alone society. Let me tell you, our society is completely upside down today. We are being controlled by fear. Who wants to live their life that way? I sure do not! In fact, I refuse to live in fear! That does not mean being an asshole, rude, or belligerent. It means living your truth while respecting other people's truth. We can love all people, but sometimes we just need to love them from a distance. Respect for yourself and respect for others is a goal I am constantly working on. I believe it is a lifelong journey that gets easier and easier the more we recognize and work on it.

Does that mean our goal is perfection? No! That is not a goal because we already are perfect. It always breaks my heart a little when I hear people say, "Well, nobody's perfect!" or "I'm only human!" To me, that sets you up for a lifetime of judgment against yourself as well as others around you. The thing is, we have no right to judge anyone else. We do not know why they are here in human form for this lifetime. The example I love to use because it is a bit over the top is that suppose some person decided to come to Earth to experience what it is like to be the biggest A-hole on the planet. We could say they are really doing a wonderful job! They are doing it perfectly! We cannot judge them for being contrary, a pain in the backside, or an awful human being because they are doing exactly what they came here to do! You must trust that you too are living your life perfectly. You might not be the person you want to be. You might not be living the life you want to live, but, trust me, you are living your life perfectly. You have the right to change who you are and how you express yourself; but everything you have been through, the good, the bad, and the ugly, brought you to where you are today. That is worth everything. You would not be who you are and doing what you are doing without those experiences.

For those of you who have experienced trauma and abuse in your past might be wondering what this means for you. You have spent most of your life trying to figure out why these things happen to you. You might feel stuck or that life dealt you a hand that is just not fair. You might feel trapped by your past. Still, the situations you have experienced brought you to where you are today. You had a harder start than most people, but that does not mean you cannot change and have a life you want or only dreamed about. When we are stuck and not living the life we want, we are judging other people. We are judging others for our situation, and that is not fair. You are giving your power away to someone else by judging them and what they did to you. Not fair? Maybe. Unchangeable? No! You are not responsible for the abuse you suffered when you were young, but you are responsible for healing yourself as an adult.

We can only judge ourselves. We cannot let anyone else judge us. If we do, we are giving our power away. We are letting their opinions matter. We are letting others dictate who we are and how we live our lives. I do not know about you, but I am way too busy to let other people's opinions dictate who I am and how I behave. Is change easy? Sometimes yes and sometimes no.

I need to tell you about an experience I had many years ago. During the night, I was taken to the other side to meet with my council of elders. What is a council of elders you might ask? It is my understanding, as well as using the words of St. Germain and Jane Halliwell, that a council of elders is a group of high vibrating souls dedicated to one soul per council. The council works with our spirit guides, angels, and masters to assist us in living the life we came here to live. Very few people realize they have this council and how deeply loved and guided they are by their council.

The council of elders is also responsible for your life review, which is where the judging comes in and is where my experience with my council of elders picks up.

One night, I was taken to the other side, or at least, it did not feel like anything I had ever experienced here on Earth. The main council member, who felt somehow different from my main guide, introduced me to my council. They all looked like old men resembling Obi-Wan Kenobi, wearing brown cloak-like items as robes. I was not sure why I was there but did not feel in danger. It felt odd and certainly not something I had ever experienced in this lifetime. I was then put in a clear circular tube, which felt like the old ATM booths – also very much like a round aquarium and I was the fish looking out from the inside. As soon as I was inside the pseudo-ATM machine, holographic images began appearing on the walls. These images were of times in my life when I had unkind thoughts, deeds, and actions towards others. The thing is, these thoughts, deeds, and actions were not what I would have expected. They were not the obvious things where we have regrets later and apologize to the person we offended. The one image that stands out to me was when I was back in high school and waiting for the bus to take me home. As I sat on the stone wall waiting, a girl I did not even know walked in front of me on the sidewalk on her way home. The only thing I remember thinking was – ooo, she has icky hair. This was something very typical of someone in high school, and I did not give it a second thought.

That is it, the only negative thought I had as I then boarded the bus home. Who knew that some 40 years later I would be shown that scene? What came with that image, however, were the emotions of that girl who passed by me, who was the recipient of my negative thought. My less than generous thought stayed with her and has affected her entire life! I felt so ashamed that I almost cried and would have given just about anything to take back that thought from so long ago.

Here is the thing: I was not being judged by my council of elders. I was judging myself. My council of elders was simply showing me things from my past, but I was doing the judging. Believe me, I was a harsh judge. When the images were finished being presented to me, I felt a failure as a human being. I felt cruel, unjust, and mean. I started to leave the ATM booth but was stopped by the elder in charge. He telepathically spoke to me and told me to wait – we were not finished. I was so humbled and ashamed that I did not think I could take anymore. I did not even know how I could begin to rectify what I had done, let alone turn my life around.

I was asked to please stay in the booth and watch some more images. Things changed, to my relief. I was now being shown images of where I had good thoughts, deeds, and actions. Once again, these were not obvious, such as giving money to a homeless person or volunteering at certain organizations as I had done most of my life. These were as subtle in a positive way as the negative thought I had about the high school student. These were thoughts and deeds I did not even remember doing. I cannot list an example because I truly do not remember them even happening. The images showed me that I had done many good things in my life that affected people in a positive way their entire life – without their knowing and without me knowing.

By the end of the session of positive images, I felt relieved and assured I had not failed at life completely. As I judged myself, I also graded myself with a solid B on the scale of ABCDF. I felt much better about the person I was, but knew I still had a long way to go. The main message of this session was that, truly, even the thoughts we have affect people in ways we cannot imagine and just being nice to a person can give them the life or encouragement they need to go on another day or even the rest of their life. How powerful is that?

The council did not praise me for the positive things just as they did not judge me for the negative. They showed me the images, and I made the judgment myself. This was a life review that many of us have heard about but have no idea what it is all about. I can tell you that it is painful and humiliating beyond belief. The council did not judge, but they were certainly witnesses. The idea that there was someone witnessing my every thought, deed, and action brought me to my knees.

At that very moment, my life changed. I became more cognizant of my thoughts as well as my actions. I have become aware now of how my very thoughts can and do affect people. That does not mean I do not have negative thoughts – I do. That does not mean I do not do negative things – I do. I just hope I do fewer and fewer as the years progress and I learn and remember more. After all, just like you, I am in the human experience to learn how my actions affect others but also to use my lifetime to remember who I am in spirit. Even if my positive thoughts and actions far outweigh the negative, the negative is still there. I am human after all... just like you. I am striving to be my best self...just like you. I now have a better understanding of what a life review looks like and, more importantly, what it feels like.

My council members asked me, when this experience was complete, how I felt. There really were no words. It was an awakening? Enlightening? Shocking? Thrilling? I think the best word is humbling. I am still trying to understand that word and define in my life. Humbling should not be shaming; it should help you realize that we are all so powerful as spirits and as human beings and that what we say and do does affect other people in a most incredible and profound way. We need to learn to use that power to help our fellow humans who are struggling too…just like us.

Part Two

"Love one another and help others to rise to the higher levels, simply by pouring out love. Love is infectious and the greatest healing energy."

- Sai Baba

Alternative Healing Modalities

There are approximately 70 different alternative healing modalities that are known in our modern world. I am not going to address all of them, but I am going to talk about 22 of them. As we all know, different people respond to different things, including alternative healing modalities. What works for you might not work for someone else. What works for someone else might not work for you. That is why there are so many options; you can discover what your body and mind respond to and what helps you heal. I will be listing 22 different modalities with a brief description of each. It is then up to you to do the research to find the right practitioner for you who specializes in that modality. Some practitioners work in person only. Others can work remotely – long distance energy work. I have experienced both in-person and remote sessions and will tell you that both are equally effective. Personally, I have experienced several of the modalities in the following chapters.

Acupressure –

Acupressure is like acupuncture in that it is based on the concept of energy, which flows through the meridians of the body. There are certain pressure points in the body that unlock energy blocks in that area as well as other blocked areas in the body. It is an effective form of stimulation to help the muscles relax and, therefore, allow movement and improvement in the affected areas of the body. A meridian is simply an energy highway throughout the body.

Acupuncture –

Acupuncture is like acupressure but with the addition of needles in certain meridians. The insertion of those very thin needles is through a person's skin at specific points in the body and at various depths. The practitioner activates the needles in specific gentle movements. The needles are meant to stimulate the energy flow of the body, reducing blocks and reducing or eliminating pain.

Aromatherapy –

Aromatherapy is a holistic treatment using natural plant extracts. It enhances both physical and emotional health. Many people use aromatherapy with essential oils applied directly to the skin or through a diffuser. You do need to research which oil to use and whether it can be applied directly or not. Many oils are so strong that they can create a reaction to the skin. Many people will mix the oil with what is called a carrier oil to reduce the potency when applied directly. Using a diffuser will filter the oil with water throughout the room for several hours.

Bach Flower Therapy –

Bach flower products are made from watered down extracts from the flowers of wild plants. Edward Bach, a medical doctor and homeopath, created these remedies in the early 1900s. Bach believed that healing negative emotions helps the body heal itself. His system contains 38 remedies that each address a specific negative emotion.

Cranial Sacral Therapy-

Cranial Sacral Therapy uses a series of gentle techniques to remove blocks and restore a subtle movement, or pulse, in the central nervous system.

Crystal Healing –

I personally love crystals. They come from the Earth and, in my opinion, bring the healing qualities of the Earth with them. The practice of using crystals is borrowed from Hinduism and Buddhism. People are drawn to their colors and beauty, whether they are polished or in their raw state. It is common practice to use stones or crystals whose colors are aligned with the colors of the chakras. There are hundreds of other stones with each having their own meaning and energies. You can carry your stones with you in your pockets or leave them laying around your house or office, letting their powers help you in everyday life with mindfulness and reflection.

Hypnotherapy –

Hypnotherapy is a form of therapy that can be used to reprogram the subconscious mind, create a heightened sense of learning, or explore past lives and lives between lives. Many people are hesitant to be hypnotized because they might have seen or heard of stage hypnosis, which is quite different. Stage hypnosis is used for entertainment purposes and is not what I am addressing today. Hypnotherapy is meant to help stop smoking, weight loss, eliminate phobias, and explore your past lives. You are always aware of who you are and are always in control – you just have clarity in your mind that gives you the ability to recall trauma or the origin of addictive behavior and release it.

Hellerwork –

Hellerwork is a system of bodywork that combines deep tissue massage, body movement education, and verbal dialog. It is designed to realign the body's structure for overall health, improvement of posture, and reduction of physical and mental health. I've personally gone through the eleven recommended sessions of Hellerwork and can attest to the realignment of my own body.

Massage –

In massage therapy, a certified and trained professional manipulates the soft tissues of your body –

muscle, connective tissue, tendons, ligaments, and skin. The massage therapist uses varying degrees of pressure and movement to the comfort level of the client. There are several different kinds of massage as well: Swedish, cupping, tantric, deep tissue, lymphatic, shiatsu, and Thai. Just ask your therapist which options they offer and make your decision from there.

Music or Sound Therapy –

Music or sound therapy deconstructs music into pure sound. Sound can have such a powerful effect on our emotions and the vibrations of our bodies. We all resonate to different sounds and vibrations, and a sound therapy session will speak to your soul song or sound to connect with your body's personal vibration. This connection can align with your soul and your body, keeping you in perfect balance. My personal experience comes from two different practitioners. One sings in ancient languages through a drum. The sound echoes and reverberates through the room and the body. The other practitioners I have worked with have an entire room filled with gongs, bowls, chimes, and even a didgeridoo. You get completely immersed in the sound as your soul song is sung in complete harmony with your body. Sound therapy is an amazing alternative form of healing, and I recommend it for anyone.

New Thought –

New Thought is under the umbrella of Metaphysics or things beyond the physical. New Thought is a collection of various religious communities based on idealism, optimism, and common ideals coming together using the expression of spirituality. Although founded early in the 19th century, it was in the 1950s when momentum was gaining and New Thought really became part of the public consciousness. New Thought followers believe that God, Source, The Creator is everywhere and exists in everything, that your thoughts create your reality. New Thought is also known as the New Age Movement.

Nutritional Healing –

Nutritional healing is an alternative way of taking care of the body with the foods we eat. The belief is that, by nourishing the body in the right way, you get to the root of imbalances in the body. I highly recommend the book *Prescription for Nutritional Healing* by Phyllis Balch. I personally have owned this book for a few decades now and have always found the information to be helpful and insightful.

Nutritional Supplements –

Nutritional supplements are any dietary supplement you might use to lower your risk of health problems. They can contain herbs, minerals, and vitamins. With the Western diet, many of us are not getting the nutrition we need out of the food we eat, so we add supplements to assist in getting the nutrition. In addition to eating the right foods and exercising, supplements can be effective in maintaining a healthy body and lifestyle.

Pilates –

Pilates is a form of exercise and physical movement to stretch, strengthen, and balance the body according to PMA, the Pilates Method Alliance. First invented in the 1920s by Joseph Pilates, Pilates has now hit the mainstream and become a household name. With consistent practice of certain exercises combined with breathing, Pilates has been found to be an important part of physical fitness as well as physical rehabilitation.

Reflexology –

Reflexology is the art of applying pressure to areas of the feet, hands, and ears. It is based on the theory that these parts of the body are connected to various organs. Imbalances or the flow of energy in the body are thought to be the precursor to illness. Therefore, by massaging or applying pressure to the parts of the body associated with organs, it is thought that energy and, therefore, balance will be restored to the body.

Reiki –

Reiki is a type of alternative healing therapy developed in Japan in the late 1800s. The thought behind Reiki is to take universal energy through the practitioners' hands and into the body of the client. I am a Reiki master and can attest to the results of using Reiki on a regular basis. Reiki is used for relaxation and moving energy around in the body to remove energy blocks, allowing the body to heal itself.

Rolfing –

Rolfing structural integration is a form of bodywork that reorganizes the connective tissues, called fascia, that permeate the entire body. Although I've never tried Rolfing, my research has told me that it is very similar to Hellerwork. See which is available in your community and do your own research to help you make the decision that is best for you.

Self-Hypnosis –

Self-hypnosis is a form of hypnosis performed by the individual rather than by a practitioner or hypnotherapist and is commonly used for concentration, relaxation, and motivation. It is the art of becoming highly focused and giving yourself positive suggestions or affirmations, usually with a specific goal in mind.

Spiritual Mind Treatment –

Spiritual Mind Treatment stems from the work of Ernest Holmes and The Science of Mind. It believes in and teaches the concept that there is one universal presence of which each of us is a part. It is becoming aware of the God presence within and realizing that which we want is already ours.

Support Groups –

I founded a support group in 2018 for individuals who have experienced alien contact. I belonged to a similar support group almost 25 years before and realized the understanding and support of others with a similar mindset was invaluable in being understood and heard. There are support groups that exist for almost anything that happens in life. The idea behind them is to give an individual a chance to talk about their experiences without judgment of any kind and receive constructive information from others in the group with similar experiences. It is always a safe place to be yourself and be vulnerable without judgment from others.

Traditional Chinese Medicine –

Traditional Chinese medicine (TCM) has evolved over the years but has mostly stayed with traditional beliefs and can include acupuncture, tai chi as well as herbal products to address various health problems. The basic idea is that TCM works with energy blocks in the body through the chakras and other meridians, helping to restore energy movement so the body can heal itself.

Yoga –

Yoga consists of specific poses with focus on the breath. It is a combination of physical and mental exercises that have existed for thousands of years. Ten poses make up a complete yoga workout. Yoga can help keep your back and joints healthy, improve your overall health, strengthen your muscles, improve your balance, and improve your overall health.

Whether you choose one or more of these types of alternative healing modalities, you should be able to find a benefit. I have tried almost all mentioned and have found, what I like to call, a golden nugget in all of them. I respond to some better than others, but all have given me a benefit of some kind. I liken it to reading a variety of books. You might find one that does not resonate with you at the time, so you put it back on the shelf for the time being. It might be two years later when you open it again and find that every word now makes sense to you. Other books might not mean much to you except for something as small as one sentence. But that one sentence made your day or altered your thinking in a profound way. I treasure almost every book I have read just as I have treasured every form of alternative healing. I have benefited from every session and am grateful for the experience.

Journaling

I have been journaling for the past 25 years. Like many young girls, I made many attempts at keeping a diary, which usually lasted about three days. I did not have the discipline nor the life experiences to be able to keep it up. But, about 25 years ago I was laid off from a job I loved. Of course, I went into a deep depression and was questioning who I was and what value I brought to this planet. After a couple weeks of self-pity, I decided I had had enough of listening to myself whine and feel sorry for myself, so I pick up the book *The Artist's Way* by Julia Cameron. This was one of many books that completely changed my life. This is an at-home, three-month course with exercises to do every day, every week, and every month. I put my head down and got to work, knowing I was a creative personality with the hope and expectation that this book would help me find my way.

Not only did this book help me find my way, but it also turned my world upside down. I will not go into all the ways this book influenced me, but journaling was one of the ways in which Julia refers to as morning pages. I was required to write three pages of longhand writing each day. I must confess that some mornings, my pages read something like this – I do not know what to write about today. I am so bored, and life is dismal. What shall I do with my day? Nap? Cry? Scream?

On other days, however, I was inspired and felt creative, motivated, and happy. I discovered that the more I did the morning pages, the easier they were to write, the less depressed I became, and the more frequent were my happy days. The morning pages became such a part of my being that, after the three-month class was completed, I felt a bit empty. I felt like something was missing. After a period, I was back at work and in a routine that did not allow for writing time every morning, so I developed the habit of journaling once a week. I now reserve Sunday mornings for writing and only writing. Everything else can wait. For 25 years, I have kept up this habit. I did notice that my writing was generally filled with venom in the first two years of journaling. I was a bit horrified that those words and thoughts were coming out of my head, through my hand, and onto the paper. I also noticed, however, that I had less of a need to dump on my friends when the venom was put down on paper. Catty things that might have come out of my mouth before were now reserved for my private journal. After a couple of years, I noticed that there were fewer and fewer pages of diatribe or negativity. My words were becoming introspective on the paper, which led to more thoughtfulness towards myself and others. It was the cheapest therapy I could imagine! The cost was $15 a year for my journal and a couple of hours a week at home….in my bed…drinking decaf coffee…in my pjs. Yes, I could certainly keep this up! Now, every Sunday I can hardly wait to get my journal out and begin writing. It is fun to see how the writings have morphed over the years. I now have conversations with my spirit guides through the writings. I ask the hard questions and will almost always get an answer in my head while I am still writing the question! My Sunday mornings are MY time and are so incredibly peaceful that I cannot imagine giving up that time or my therapeutic journaling.

So, what can journaling do for you? First, journaling is just one way of finding yourself and your peace. There are so many ways to start or continue your spiritual journey. I have found journaling to be something I now HAVE to have in my life. There might be something else that resonates better for you, but you will have to figure that out for yourself. I do recommend at least trying to journal. And by trying, I mean for at least three months – and at least once a week. If it still does not resonate with you, move on to something else.

Here are some of the benefits I have found from journaling:

1. Time to myself
2. Time to reflect
3. The ability to put my anger and hurt on paper rather than passing it on to friends
4. Connecting to my spirit guides in a different way
5. Stimulating my creativity
6. Recapping the week with everything to which I am thankful
7. If it was not a great week – why? Is there something I could have done differently?
8. Time to plan

These are just a few benefits from journaling. I am certain that you will find other benefits unique to you. Isn't it worth giving it a shot?

Let us get down to basics. Silly as this may sound, the hardest part of journaling for me was finding the right journal! Some were too big and hard to handle from the comfort of my bed. Others were bound too tight, so I could not write all the way to the inside margin (I know, sounds silly, but sometimes it is the little things that keep you from pursuing something great!).

I finally found the perfect journal for me. It is spiral bound so I can easily write to any margin. It has the right number of pages so I can fill at least four pages each week. Many times, I feel like journaling mid-week or more than four pages on Sundays. There are always enough extra pages to allow me to do this. My perfect journal always has exactly the right number of pages for me to write to my heart's content and never run out of paper or have too many blank pages at the end of the year.

What I am trying to say is that finding your perfect journal will be trial and error. You might find that a loose-leaf notebook works for you. You can add paper and pages as you need them. You might find that, if you have a huge journal, you can fit in more than one year. Stay with it – do not give up until you find your perfect journal to fit your perfect schedule while you create your perfect life.

Astrology

Astrology is the art of studying the zodiac. There are 12 signs in the zodiac. Each sign comes with its certain strengths and weaknesses to help define a person's basic personality, character, preferences, and fears. Each zodiac sign is influenced by planetary placements and positions, which are occurring at the moment of birth.

Each of the 12 zodiac signs is divided into one of four elements: fire, earth, air, and water. The elements represent certain energies that influence us and are alive in all of us. They also help us have a better understanding of our potential and positive traits as well as the less desirable traits.

Listed below are the four elements and some of the associated personality traits as well as the zodiac signs.

Water Signs – Cancer (June 21- July 22), Scorpio (October 23 – November 21), and Pisces (February 19 – March 20)

Water signs are emotional and sensitive. They are also very intuitive and creative and can be mysterious too – still waters run deep. They love deep and intimate conversations and will be loyal and always support loved ones.

Fire Signs – Aries (March 21 - April 19), Leo (July 23 - August 22), and Sagittarius (November 22 - December 21)

Fire signs are dramatic, passionate, and temperamental. They anger quickly but get over it just as fast. They are intelligent, self-aware, and idealistic people who are already ready for action.

Earth Signs – Taurus (April 20 - May 20), Virgo (August 23 - September 22), and Capricorn (December 22 - January 19)

Earth signs are the people who keep us grounded. They are down to earth folks who are also conservative and realistic. They can also be very emotional.

Air Signs – Gemini (May 21 - June 20), Libra, (September 23 - October 22), and Aquarius (January 20 - February 18)

Air signs are social and love communication and relationships with other people. They are philosophical and love a good book. They are friendly and enjoy giving advice but are also great thinkers.

Astrology claims that nothing happens by accident or is a coincidence and helps us understand ourselves and the world around us. It can help us make good decisions for future success.

The Earth is in a certain position when we are born. This determines your astrological sign. Where other planets are aligned can also determine major influences in our personalities.

If you are thinking of having your astrological chart done, make sure you find a reputable astrologer. They will need the exact date, year, time, and place of your birth to give you the most accurate reading. This makes each person's chart uniquely theirs.

There are also certain signs that are more compatible than others. If you are considering a love relationship, it might behoove both of you to get your charts done. There is much more to astrology than just your sun sign (the sign under which you were born). A good astrologer can help you decipher the influences in both of your charts, your obstacles, dreams, and goals. A good astrologer can also help you understand your chart to determine your career and education too. In other words, astrology can be a blueprint to your life!

Many people read their daily horoscope, which is derived from astrology, for guidance. This is fun but should be looked at as something broad. A daily horoscope does not know you or the other planets that influence you from the moment of your birth.

I have chosen to touch on a few highlights of astrology since it would take an entire book to really teach the intricate nuances. Astrology is both an art and a science and takes years to really understand. With computer programs anyone can create a chart, but it takes a very gifted astrologer to be able to decipher the information and deliver it in a way that really assists the person getting the reading.

Numerology

Like an astrological chart, a numerology chart is your personalized guide to life. It reveals strengths, weaknesses, and who you could become if you use your chart as a guide.

There are six important numbers in your numerology chart:

1. Your soul number
2. Your personality number
3. Your power name number
4. Your birthday number
5. Your life path number
6. Your attitude number

So, what does each number mean? I have tried to learn numerology but must admit, I struggle with finding the time, figuring it all out, etc. What works best for me and might work best for you is to find a good numerologist and have the experts do the work! I will visit my favorite numerologist once or twice a year or if I am planning a special event and need to know if the date of the event lines up with my intentions. More than once, I have had to change my plans!

Here are the basic meanings of the six different numbers:

The soul number – This describes what you feel inside. These are your inner urges and desires. This number is what makes your soul happy. Others may not see this side of you, but you will feel it.

The personality number – This describes the parts and pieces of yourself that you show to others. It describes how others perceive you and what you show to the world.

The power number – This describes the strength of your name and your character.

The birthday number – This describes how others see you.

The life path number – This describes the path you must take for you to be happy. It is your core identity of who you really are. This is the most important number in your chart!

The attitude number – This describes your general attitude towards life. This is also a particularly important number, second only to your life path number!

How do you figure out your numbers? Well, the numbers are one through nine and added together. I will use myself as an example. My birthday is July 8, 1955. So, I add 7 (month), 8 (day), and 1,9,5,5 (year).

The first step looks like this: 7+8 = 15, 1+9+5+5 = 20

Second step looks like this: 15+20 = 35

Third step looks like this: 3+5 = 8

My life-path number is 8.

Whenever you have a number that is two digits, those two must be added together to create the single digit.

Each number has significant meaning and has positive influences in addition to challenges. Here is a brief breakdown of the positive as well as the challenges for each number.

One –

Positive – Leadership, innovation, independence

Challenges – Overly critical, defensive, inner turmoil

Two –

Positive – Sensitive, cooperative, peacemaker

Challenges – Whiny, martyr, anger

Three –

Positive – Optimism, charm, self-expression

Challenges – Conformity, manic-depression, mood swings

Four –

Positive – Organized, honest, hard worker

Challenges – Future oriented, not living in the present, too much in their own heads

Five –

Positive – Adventurous, change, freedom

Challenges – Addiction, drama, overkill

Six –

Positive – Responsible, harmony, nurturing

Challenges – Overbearing, controlling, negative

Seven –

Positive – Intelligent, intuitive, observing

Challenges – Loner, escapism, addiction

Eight –

Positive – Successful, leader, strength

Challenges – Greed, workaholic, fearful of loss

Nine –

Positive – Idealistic, compassionate, healer

Challenges – Blame others, cannot let go, feeling neglected

Although numerology is simple math, math has never been my strong suit, so I prefer to go to the experts. The experts really understand numbers and can interpret them, especially for you. There are many hidden nuances that only an expert can interpret. I am not saying do not try it; do try it! The more you can learn, the more tools you have in your toolbox for understanding who you are and why you are here on the planet.

So much of what we do and what we say is driven by our unconscious. We were born on a particular day for a reason: so our birth date number would help us achieve what we came here to achieve. We were given a particular name for the same reason. Our soul wants to help us in a plethora of ways, one of those ways is numerology.

Akashic Records

According to Wikipedia, the definition of Akashic Records is this: "In theosophy and anthroposophy, the Akashic Records are a compendium of all universal events, thoughts, words, emotions, and intent ever to have occurred in the past, present, or future in terms of all entities and life forms, not just human. They are believed by theosophists to be encoded in a non-physical plane of existence known as the mental plane." It is believed all thoughts, words, intent etc. generates its own unique "frequency" or "vibration," which is stored in the Akashic Records.

In my own experience and understanding, the Akashic Records are a library with records of everything that has ever been or ever will be. Basically, I am saying the same thing as Wikipedia but in a condensed form.

My first experience with the Akashic Records happened by accident. I did not know what the Akashic Records were. In fact, I had never even heard the words Akashic Records. I was meditating one morning when I found myself wandering through this vast library. There were floor-to-ceiling books on shelves of deep brown wood. There were tables where scholars were sitting, reading, and studying who knows what. There was a check out area of sorts. I was not allowed to read any of the books without permission from the librarian on duty, so I walked up to the checkout counter and asked for my book. After just seconds, she lifted a huge book on to the counter. This book had a spine of around a foot wide. The book had the look of an old law book you might see on the bottom shelf of a library where no one goes. It was dusty, smelled like old books, and even had loose pages threatening to fall out of the damaged spine.

I opened the book, read, and was astonished at what was there. Past lives, parallel lives, other planetary lives – you name it – it was there. I do not remember how long I read, but I do remember leaving the library without being allowed to take the book with me. As I walked out the huge wooden doors, there was a stone path camouflaged with moss, creating an otherworldly essence. It felt like fall was in the air as I walked; trees lightly blew their brightly colored leaves around me. It was warm too as I felt the fall sun warming my skin after the coolness of the library.

That memory happened sometime in my early 30s, which is now more than 30 years ago, but has stuck with me, vividly, ever since. I began researching by asking my spiritual teachers what it was that I had experienced. They quickly told me it was the Akashic Records, but they were surprised that I had visited them without even knowing what they were. I had my answer, or so I thought. Many years later, I discovered a book written by Linda Howe called *How to Read the Akashic Records*. Since that first book, she has written several others on the Akashic Records, all of which I highly recommend. That book renewed my interest in the subject, and I tried to access the records using Linda's instructions.

Quickly, I found myself back in the library. This time was a bit different, however. I wandered through the library and knew I had to go to the front desk to find "my" book. After my book was lifted to the counter, I was able to open it once again, only this time, I was in for a huge surprise! When I opened the book, it became a pop-up book of sorts. As I opened the still deteriorating spine, what appeared to be a multi-layered clear chess game popped up. I could see from the top down all the different clear layers of this chess board. What it was, I discovered, was a representation of my different human lives. Imagine, if you will, many, many layers of glass stacked on top of each other with what felt like three inches in between each layer. As I looked from the top down, I saw myself living different lives. I was female in some, male in others, and had changed roles from life to life. For instance, in one life I might have been a mother, in another a grandfather, in another a child, and in another a teenager. This went on and on and on, as far as I could see through the many layers of glass.

The part I had a hard time wrapping my head around was that, if one of "me" in a life did something utilizing free will, it affected the lives of all the other lives I was living. You see, if there is no time on the other side, we really cannot have past lives, can we? These are all parallel lives – all happening at the same time. Since we do interact with many of the same souls life after life, one of us doing something using free will can change the life plan of not only that life but all the other lives being lived by that soul and all the other soul's experiences of the other lives. Whew! Crazy! The major life lessons will not change, but the way we go about learning or expressing them will change depending on what the other lives are doing and deciding. This is all happening simultaneously! Believe me, it makes my head hurt just thinking about it, let alone trying to explain it. While I was visiting the Akashic Records and looking down through the many glass-layered lives, it made perfect sense and was completely enlightening! After leaving the records and coming back to the life I know and am living now, it blew my mind and continues to blow my mind every time I think about it.

In my practice as a psychic medium, I have had a few people ask me if I can access the Akashic Records. I do tell them that, yes, I can access them, but that is certainly not my strength. There are other practitioners that access the records as the main part of their practice, and I recommend they go visit them. If they want an answer to a few past life questions, I am definitely capable of doing that. One example came from a gentleman I was reading. He wanted to connect with an old friend of his who had recently passed. His friend came to me loud and clear and gave a few messages. She then went into detail that she was working with the Akashic Records on the other side! She was the spirit standing behind the desk that has shown up every time for me when I have visited. She worked there part of the time and was one of the many spirits who would collect the "books" for the individuals wanting information about their current or past lives. She loved her job and was thrilled to get back to it as that is what she always did between lives here on Earth…she worked at the Akashic Records.

I have always known that we work and have jobs on the other side, but I had no idea until then that working with the Akashic Records could be one of those jobs! I guess it is very much like life on Earth; we all have jobs to do, including being a librarian, which is exactly what this lady's job was with the Akashic Records.

If you have an interest in learning how to access the records, I recommend that you read any book by Linda Howe, take a class online or in person, or ask your guides to take you there during one of your meditations. If you are supposed to be there, they will show you the way.

I also recommend when you visit the records that you go prepared with questions you have about your current life, past lives, or even family issues. It will be easier for you to access the endless information available to you through the records. You might even want to consider asking for a tour of the library before you ask for your own book. You might see scholars sitting at large wooden tables reading. You might see other spirits walking up and down all the rows of books.

The atmosphere is a calm that you have never experienced, but you can smell the dust of the ages of the library itself and the timeless books. At least, that has been my experience. As you know, everyone experiences things differently and in a way that most resonates with their own healing and highest good. When you are ready, go to the front desk and ask for your book of life. I have been told that the books are not allowed to leave the library, however. You must read your book at the front desk or at one of the beautiful tables inside the library. That is why I think it is important to have any questions or concerns ready before you enter.

Also, know that you can ask about one life or keep it more general and ask the most important thing you need to know affecting your life today. I always like that question. We are affected and driven by unseen forces. Many times, the only way we recognize that behavior is when we find ourselves repeating...Oh, I have always been forgetful, or I have never been lucky, or I have always been clumsy. On the other side, you might say, I have always been good at music – it just comes naturally to me. My favorite is, I was born dancing! I cannot imagine life without dance, music, art, etc. These are all things from past lives that are affecting you positively or negatively in this life! We usually do not pay much attention to the positive things – we tend to take those things for granted. It is the so-called negative things of which we want to rid or have a better understanding.

Wouldn't it be fun to visit the Akashic Records with the question of where did I get my gift of...? Or on the flip side, I would really like to understand why I have two left feet. I can barely walk a straight line, let alone dance! You will get the answers and clarification to all your questions if you take the time and have the patience to understand you. If something shows up in the records from a past life that no longer serves you in this life, you can release it and let it go. You can be grateful for the things that continue to serve you well in this life, but you do not have to be burdened with things that no longer serve you. Release them, let them go, and then continue living your life now the way you want to. You are the creator of your own life. That includes letting go of things of which you might not even have been aware before your visit to the amazing Akashic Records.

I have always believed information is power. We all know things from our childhood in this current life continue to affect us, so why wouldn't things from past lives affect us too? Once we take the time to learn and study, we have more power in this life to be the person we want to be, live the life we want to live, and continue to grow and flourish in love and light instead of confusion and frustration.

When we choose to create our lives and live-in love and light, we also free up energy to help others. Isn't that also why we are all here? I believe it is to serve others. How can we do that authentically if we are all wrapped up in our own stuff. Just like the airlines say in an emergency, put your oxygen mask on first and then help your child or others needing assistance. You must take care of you first so you can be of better assistance to others. You are the one awakening to the beauty and power and wonder of the universe! Learn as much as you can. Discover who you are! Share that knowledge with others so they can awaken and help others too. What a wonderful world we live in now. Can you just imagine the possibilities if we all healed our own wounds so we can assist others in healing theirs?

Divination Tools

Divination tools are items that psychics and mediums use to seek information, guidance, and knowledge to be used to guide and inform clients. The information comes from the spirit world and is transmitted through the tool to the psychic. There are many divination tools, but I am going to address the 11 most popular tools today. I have used most, but not all, of these tools and find some more helpful in certain situations and others more helpful in other situations. It is up to you to try these divination tools and see if all or any work the best for you.

1. **Akashic Records** – We just talked about the Akashic Records, but here is another brief overview. There are many healing practitioners who access the Akashic Records. The Akashic Records are basically a library containing books for each soul. This Library has the record of everything that has ever been and ever will be.

2. **Angel Cards** – Of all the divination tools, Angel Cards are my personal favorite. The Angel Cards can be laid out in a variety of spreads to answer and guide the client in particular areas of their life. The information comes from the angelic realm rather than metaphysical concepts coming from different spirits. There are many different varieties of Angel Cards. You need to see which deck you are drawn to and begin learning the different meanings behind each card and how they relate to each other in any spread.

3. **Crystal Ball** – Usually, crystal balls have a reputation of being associated with charlatans in the movies and on television. I remember see-

ing on tv many crazy looking women wearing turbans, caftans, and too much make-up as they gazed into a crystal ball and delivered rather dark messages. My personal experience is more realistic. In a quiet spot and after a peaceful meditation, you ask your question and then gaze into your crystal ball. Usually, in a minute or so, you will begin to see messages within the crystal ball. It is then up to the psychic to interpret those pictures in a way that relates to the client's question.

4. **Dowsing Rods** – I first remember seeing a dowsing rod in an old western tv show where someone was trying to locate water and determine where to drill for a well. The process looked weird but so interesting to me as the "Y" shaped stick began to point toward the ground where spirit was indicating water could be found. At the time, my mind could not quite wrap around the idea that this was real. I do now own dowsing rods, which are a bit different from the "Y" shaped stick used in that old tv show. Mine are made of copper and are shaped like an "L." There are two of them, which I hold directly in front of me while I ask my questions that really need to have yes or no responses. For me, if the answer is yes, the two rods will move toward the center and form an X. If the answer is no, the rods will move away from each other. If the answer is neutral, the rods do not move at all and will stay parallel to each other. You do need to ask yes or no questions, however. The dowsing rods are my newest divination tool, and I have to say are such fun!

5. **I Ching Coins** – This is one tool that I have personally never used so am relying on research to tell you about them. These coins originated

in ancient China. Supposedly, you do not need special coins but can use other coins, such as pennies or quarters, that will have the same effect. You do need the I Ching guidebook to interpret the signs and symbols.

6. **Ouija Board** – One of the most frequently asked questions I get is, "Are Ouija boards evil?" My answer is always the same – no, they are not. They are simply a piece of board and a plastic planchette. People get the idea that they are evil from people who do not know how to safely use the board. When kids sit down to play with a Ouija board, they just ask anybody to come through for them. They do not understand the difference between high and low vibrating spirits. Before you even attempt to use a Ouija board, you must ask that only the highest vibrating spirits come through and only with information for your healing and highest good. Once you have spoken your intent, go ahead and have fun! Just always make sure your intent is pure as well. You cannot request that of spirit if your intent does not match their vibration.

7. **Pendulums** – There are so many pendulums to choose from! Where do you start? Similar to choosing crystals, pick the pendulum that you are drawn to. I have seen homemade pendulums, using an old piece of jewelry and adding a chain. Usually however, a pendulum consists of a cone shaped stone, a small length of chain, and another small metal ball or coin shaped piece at the other end of the chain. When you get your pendulum, you must first program it to your energy. You do this easily by asking the pendulum to show you a yes and then show you a no. The pendulum will swing in one direction

for a yes and the other direction for a no. You do need to ask yes or no questions for the pendulum to work.

8. **Runes** – I love runes! They were my first divination tool when I was first learning. Runes have symbols printed on small stones, tiles, or wood. I even used to make my own runes out of glass and then fire them in my kiln. They have Scandinavian origins and are used as a means of communication. You simply put the runes in a pouch, ask your question, and then pour them out. The runes that are face up are the ones you will use to answer your question. You do need a key to interpret the symbols. A key is usually included when you purchase a set of runes. The key also includes various ways to lay out the runes for specific readings.

9. **Scrying Mirrors** – Although this method is ancient and the most commonly used divination tool, it is one I personally have never used. It is simple enough to do but does require an immense amount of concentration. You simply stare into the mirror – any mirror – and ask your question. As you stare into the mirror, continue to concentrate on your question and wait for a symbol or picture of some kind to appear. This method is really a great exercise for the mind in developing concentration.

10. **Tarot Cards** – Oh my, where do I even begin?! There are hundreds of different kinds of tarot or oracle decks. Like most divination tools, you pick your deck by going in the direction your mind and body are leading you. Decks almost always come with a guide or explanation on how to use them, which does make it easier. Each guide offers several different "spreads" or ways to lay

out the cards, depending on what you want to know. Each card has a meaning, but it can be interpreted in different ways, depending on where the card is in your spread and which cards are next to it. It can take years of study to really get to know your cards, but what a fun way to learn! To me, the most effective way to use your cards is to incorporate them with your intuition. Their different meanings can make much more sense using your intuition.

11. **Teacups** – This is another tool that I do not have personal experience with. You do not use just ordinary teacups; you must use specially made teacups that have symbols and patterns printed on the inside. After you have brewed your loose tea, you must drink it until all that is left in the bottom of the cup are the leftover leaves. By observing the patterns and images that the leaves make and using your intuition and experience, you can interpret the messages.

Summary

Where do you go from here? You have been experiencing some strange things and want to know more, or you have had your interest peaked in the paranormal and metaphysics and want to know what all the fuss is about.

No matter the circumstances, I am so glad you have read this book as an introduction to the world of metaphysics (beyond the physical). So where do you go from here? You start by trusting your gut instincts! Which chapter or chapters caught your attention the most? That is where you start! Whichever chapter or subject matter made your gut go hmmmm, that is where you want to further your research and dig deeper. You can do that by going online to learn more, taking online classes, or booking a session with a practitioner skilled in that modality. I will warn you that there are many charlatans out there, so please beware! In my opinion, the best way to find the perfect practitioner for you is by word of mouth. Ask your friends whom they have gone to see. That is usually your best bet.

There are also metaphysical expos in most major cities. Practitioners will offer shortened sessions at their booth, usually at a reduced price. It is the perfect place to try out several different modalities in one day to get a taste of what the modality is like and if you connect with the practitioner. If you do and you get a good reading in that short amount of time, it is usually a good investment to book a full session.

The best way to spot a charlatan is if they try to "up-sell" you. What that means is if they use fear to get you to spend more money with them. The minute you hear the word curse or spell or something along those lines – run! Get out of there as fast as you can. The practitioner is not going to hurt you in any way except through your wallet. Do not fall for it. Trust your gut, as I mentioned earlier. If your gut tells you something does not feel quite right, it is true. That is the real start to your metaphysical journey – to trust yourself first and foremost. Once you have got that down, then you can begin to trust the process of metaphysics. Practitioners are there to guide you on your path to you. To help you remember who you are, who you came here to be, and what you want to learn and experience. No other reason.

I always say that I can read other people, usually with no problem. But…I get stuck on my own stuff! Every good metaphysical practitioner should have someone they work with to keep them on their own path too! My goal is to be the best version of me that I can be. That means work every single day. I get stuck just like everybody else, so I have a few practitioners skilled in different modalities that I go to on a regular basis. They shed light on my "stuckness" and help me to see the light. It not only helps me in my life, but it makes me a better practitioner.

Never stop learning. Never stop growing. Never stop expanding. You are here to remember who you are in spirit form. Society, friends, and family have no business telling you who you are, what you should be, and where you should go. That is your decision only. You can travel that path alone or you can go to the experts who can give you the tools to help you achieve what you came here to achieve. They can give you the tools, but it is up to you to use those tools. Use the tools or remain where you are today. The choice is yours. It is always yours. Are you ready? Buckle up Buttercup! Get ready for the most joyous journey you will ever take. The journey back to you.

Blessings to you all,

Kristi

Resource Guide

Any books by Dolores Cannon
Any books by Rebecca Rosen
Any books by Gary Zukav

Adventures of the Soul – James Van Praagh
The Afterlife of Billy Fingers – Annie Kagan
The Alchemist – Paulo Coelho
A New Earth – Eckhart Tolle
Answers About the Afterlife – Bob Olson
A Return to Love – Marianne Williamson
The Artist's Way – Julia Cameron
The Art of Happiness – Dalai Lama XIV
Autobiography of a Yogi – Paramahansa Yogananda

Becoming Supernatural – Dr. Joe Dispenza
Be Here Now – Ram Dass
Being in Balance – Dr. Wayne Dyer
Between Two Worlds – Tyler Henry
Beyond Fear – Don Miguel Ruiz
The Book of Awakening – Mark Nepo
The Book of Joy – Dalai Lama XIV and Desmond Tutu
The Book of Stones – Robert Simmons and Naisha Ahsian
The Boy Who Knew Too Much – Cathy Byrd

The Celestine Prophecy – James Redfield

Conversations with God Series – Neale Donald Walsch

Crystals for Healing – Karen Frazier

Destiny of Souls – Dr. Michael Newton

The Disappearance of the Universe – Gary R. Renard

The Divine Matrix – Gregg Braden

Dying to be Me – Anita Moorjani

Eastern Body, Western Mind – Anodea Judith

Eat, Pray, Love – Elizabeth Gilbert

The Energy Codes – Dr. Sue Morter

Essential Oils for Beginners – Althea Press

Essential Oils and Aromatherapy – Nathan Wake

Everything is Here to Help You – Matt Kahn

Expect a Miracle – Dan Wakefield

The Fifth Agreement – Don Miguel Ruiz

Final Beginnings – John Edward

The Five Levels of Attachment – Don Miguel Ruiz

The Four Agreements – Don Miguel Ruiz

Glynis Has your Number – Glynis McCants

The Happy Medium – Kim Russo

How to Read the Akashic Records – Linda Howe

I Can See Clearly Now – Dr. Wayne W. Dyer
Illuminating the Afterlife – Cyndi Dale
Inside the Other Side – Concetta Bertoldi
The Instruction – Ainslee MacLeod

The Journey After Life – Cyndi Dale
Journey of Souls – Dr. Michael Newton

Key to Yourself – Venice J. Bloodworth

Leap of Perception – Penney Peirce
Life Before Life – Jim B. Tucker
Life Between Lives – Dr. Michael Newton
Lightworker – Sahvanna Arienta
Light is the New Black – Rebecca Campbell
Linda Goodman's Love Signs – Linda Goodman
Life Visioning – Michael Bernard Beckwith
Loving What Is – Byron Katie

The Magic – Rhonda Byrne
Manifesting Michelangelo – Joseph Pierce Farrell
Many Lives, Many Masters – Dr. Brian L. Weiss
Medical Medium – Anthony William
Metaphysical Anatomy – Evette Rose
The Mastery of Love – Don Miguel Ruiz

Opening to Channel – Sanaya Roman and Duane Packer

One Last Time – John Edward

Peace is Every Step – Thich Nhat Hanh

Proof of Heaven – Eben Alexander

The Power – Rhonda Byrne

Power Crystals – John DeSalvo

The Power is Within You – Louise L. Hay

The Power of Intention – Dr. Wayne W. Dyer

The Power of Now – Eckhart Tolle

The Prophet – Kahlil Gibran

Sacred Contracts – Caroline Myss

Seth Speaks – Jane Roberts

The Seven Spiritual Laws of Success – Deepak Chopra

Siddhartha – Hermann Hesse

Signs from the Other Side – Bill Philipps

The Sleeping Prophet – Jess Stearn

Spontaneous Healing of Belief – Gregg Braden

Start Where You Are – Pema Chodron

Stillness Speaks – Eckhart Tolle

Talking to the Dead – George Noory

Unfinished Business – James Van Praagh

The Untethered Soul – Michael A. Singer

The Voice of Knowledge – Don Miguel Ruiz

Waking Up – Sam Harris

Way of the Peaceful Warrior – Dan Millman

We Are Not Alone – Kristi Pederson

Wisdom of the Ages – Dr. Wayne W. Dyer

You are Psychic – Pete A Sanders, Jr.

You Are the Universe – Deepak Chopra and Menas Kafatos

You Can't Make this Stuff Up – Theresa Caputo

Your Soul's Plan – Robert Schwartz

About The Author

Kristi is a psychic medium, author and speaker who lives in Omaha, NE. Her mission in this life is to help others stand in their own power and understand their own greatness.

Her other books are *An Extraordinary Life,* published in 2010, and *We Are Not Alone…My Extraterrestrial Contact,* published in 2019.

www.kristipederson.com

www.herextraordinarylife.net